ELLEN G. WHITE

STORY *of* HOPE

A Glimpse Into a Time When Suffering Will Be No More

REVIEW AND HERALD® PUBLISHING ASSOCIATION

Since 1861 | www.reviewandherald.com

Cover design by Gerald Lee Monks
Cover design resources from iStockphoto.com
Inside design by Aaron Troia

Copyright © 2016 by The Ellen G. White® Estate, Inc.

Published by Review and Herald® Publishing Association

Printed by Pacific Press® Publishing Association
Printed in the United States of America
All rights reserved

Unless otherwise noted, all Scripture quoted in this book is taken from
the New King James Version®. Copyright © 1982 by Thomas Nelson,
Inc. Used by permission. All rights reserved.

You can obtain additional copies of this book by calling toll-free 1-800-
765-6955 or by visiting http://www.adventistbookcenter.com.

ISBN 978-0-8280-2817-2

August 2016

Contents

Introduction

How did our world get so badly messed up? Why is there suffering? Where did evil come from? Will it ever end?

Questions such as these trouble many a thinking person. Science has no answers to them, and philosophy has many conflicting answers. Where can we find the truth?

The material in this book is selected and adapted from a larger work, *The Story of Redemption*. The author, Ellen G. White, was included among the 100 most significant Americans of all time by *Smithsonian* magazine in a special issue (Spring 2015). Her works have been translated into more than 160 languages, more than those of any other woman anywhere. Millions have benefited from her insights and inspiration.

Story of Hope is an opportunity for you to do so too.

Chapter 1

The Rebellion

In heaven, before his rebellion, Lucifer was a high and exalted angel, next in honor to God's own Son. His face, like those of the other angels, was gentle and radiated happiness. His forehead was high and broad, showing a powerful intellect. His bodily form was perfect, and his bearing was noble and majestic. A special light beamed from his face and shone around him brighter and more beautiful than around the other angels; yet Christ, God's Son, was over all the assembly of angels. He was one with the Father before the angels were created. Lucifer envied Christ, and gradually he took upon himself the command that belonged to Christ alone.

Angels acknowledged Christ as the ruler of heaven, His power and authority the same as that of God Himself. Lucifer thought of himself as a favorite in heaven among the angels. God had given him a high position, but this did not bring from him gratitude and praise to his Creator. He aspired to the height of God Himself. He gloried in his exalted status. He knew that he was honored by the angels. He had a special mission to carry out. He had been near the great Creator, and the endless beams of glorious light surrounding the eternal God had shone especially upon him. He thought how angels had obeyed his command quickly and cheerfully. Weren't his garments light and beautiful? Why should Christ be honored like this rather than himself?

He left the immediate presence of the Father, dissatisfied and filled with envy against Jesus Christ. Hiding his real purposes, he gathered the angels around him. He introduced his subject, which was himself. Like one who had been wronged,

This chapter is based on Isaiah 14:12-14,
Ezekiel 28:12-17, Revelation 12:7-9.

he talked of how God had neglected him and given preference to Jesus. He told them that from that point on, all the sweet liberty the angels had enjoyed was ended. For hadn't a ruler been appointed over them, to whom they must ever after yield slave-like honor?

He told them that he had called them together to assure them that he would no longer submit to this invasion of his rights and theirs; that never again would he bow down to Christ. Instead, he would take the honor upon himself that God should have conferred on him, and he would be the commander of all who would submit to follow him and obey his voice.

There was sharp disagreement among the angels. Lucifer and his sympathizers were trying to restructure the government of God. They rebelled against the authority of the Son.

Angels that were loyal and true tried to win this mighty, rebellious angel back to the will of his Creator. They clearly showed that Christ was the Son of God, existing with Him before the angels were created. He had always stood at the right hand of God. His gentle, loving authority had not ever been questioned before, and He had given no commands but those that it was a joy for the heavenly forces to carry out.

They urged that Christ's special honor did not detract from the honor that Lucifer had already received. The angels wept. They earnestly tried to persuade him to give up his evil design and submit to their Creator. Up to that time, they pointed out, everything had been peace and harmony. What possible reason could there be for this dissenting, rebellious voice?

Lucifer refused to listen. And then he turned from the loyal and true angels, denouncing them as slaves. These angels, true to God, stood in amazement as they saw that Lucifer was succeeding in his effort to stir up rebellion. He promised them a new and better government than they had, in which there would be complete freedom. Great numbers expressed their intent to accept him as their leader and chief commander. As he saw that his efforts were met with success, he flattered himself that he would soon have all the angels on his side, and that he would be equal with God Himself. Then all would hear *his* voice of authority commanding the entire host of heaven.

Again the loyal angels warned him, assuring him what the consequences must be if he persisted. He who could create the angels could overturn all their authority by His power and in some decisive way punish their boldness and terrible rebellion. To think that an angel should resist the law of God, which was as sacred as God Himself! They warned the rebellious to close their ears to Lucifer's deceptive arguments, and they advised him and all whom he had influenced to go to God and confess that they had been wrong for even admitting a thought of questioning His authority.

Many of Lucifer's sympathizers wanted to follow the counsel of the loyal angels and repent of their dissatisfaction and be welcomed again into the confidence of the Father and His Son. The mighty rebel then declared that he was acquainted with God's law, and if he did agree to submit and give slavish obedience, his honor would be taken from him. No more would he be entrusted with his high command. He told them that both he and they had now gone too far to go back, and he would risk the consequences, because he never would bow in servile worship to the Son of God. He claimed that God would not forgive, and now they must assert their liberty and take by force the position and authority that was not willingly given to them. In this way Lucifer, "the light-bearer," who shared God's glory, who stood next to His throne, by transgression became Satan, "the adversary."

The loyal angels hurried to the Son of God to tell Him what was taking place among the angels. They found the Father in conference with His Son, to determine how, for the best good of the loyal angels, they could forever put down the authority that Satan had claimed for himself. The great God could have hurled this arch-deceiver from heaven immediately, but this was not His intention. He would give the rebels an equal chance to test their strength and might against His own Son and His loyal angels.

In this battle every angel would choose sides, for all to see.

It would not have been safe to allow any who joined Satan in his rebellion to continue to occupy heaven. They had learned the lesson of genuine rebellion against God's unchangeable law, and this is incurable. If God had exercised His power to punish this chief rebel, discontented angels would not have been unmasked. So God took another course, because He wanted to reveal His justice and His judgment clearly to all the heavenly beings.

War in Heaven—It was the highest crime to rebel against the government of God. All heaven seemed in commotion. The angels were assigned in companies, each division with a higher commanding angel at its head. Satan was warring against the law of God, because he was ambitious to exalt himself and unwilling to submit to the authority of God's Son, heaven's great commander.

All the angels of heaven were summoned to appear before the Father. Satan unblushingly announced his dissatisfaction that Christ was honored before him. He stood up proudly and urged that he should be equal with God. Good angels wept to hear the words of Satan and his insolent boasts. God declared that the rebellious should remain in heaven no longer. They had held their high and happy existence on condition of obedience to the law that God had given to govern the high order of intelligences. But no provision had been made to save those who dared to transgress His law.

Satan grew bold in his rebellion, expressing his contempt for the Creator's law. He claimed that angels needed no law but should be left free to follow their own will, which would always guide them rightly. Law, he said, was a restriction of their liberty, and to abolish law was one great aim of his taking a stand in opposition.

The happiness of the angels consisted in their perfect obedience to law. Each had his special work assigned him, and until Satan rebelled, there had been perfect order and harmonious action in heaven.

Then there was war in heaven. The Son of God, the Prince

of heaven, and His loyal angels engaged in conflict with the arch-rebel and those who united with him. The Son of God and the true, loyal angels prevailed, and Satan and his sympathizers were expelled from heaven. All the remaining angels acknowledged and adored the God of justice. Not a taint of rebellion was left in heaven. Everything was peaceful and harmonious again, as before. Angels in heaven mourned the fate of those who had been their companions in happiness and bliss. All heaven felt their loss.

The Father consulted His Son about immediately carrying out their plan to make human beings to inhabit the earth. He would place them on probation to test their loyalty before they could be made eternally secure. They were to have the favor of God. They would talk with angels, and angels with them. God did not see fit to place them beyond the power of disobedience.

Chapter 2

The Creation

The Father and the Son began the mighty, wonderful work they had planned—of creating the world. The earth came forth from the hand of the Creator astonishingly beautiful. There were mountains and hills and plains, interspersed with rivers and bodies of water. The earth was not one extensive plain, but the sameness of the scenery was broken by hills and mountains, not high and ragged as they are now, but regular and beautiful in shape. The bare, high rocks were never visible on them, but lay beneath the surface, like bones to the earth.

The waters were evenly dispersed. The hills, mountains, and very beautiful plains were adorned with plants and flowers and tall, majestic trees of every description, which were many times larger and much more beautiful than trees are today. The air was pure and healthful, and the earth seemed like a noble palace. Angels saw this and rejoiced at the wonderful, beautiful works of God.

After they created the earth and the animals on it, the Father and Son carried out their intention, planned before the fall of Satan, to make human beings in their own image. They had worked together in the creation of the earth and every living thing upon it. And now God said to His Son, "Let us make man in our image."

As Adam came forth from the hand of his Creator, he was of noble height and beautiful symmetry. His features were perfect and beautiful. His complexion was neither white nor pale, but ruddy, glowing with the rich tint of health. Eve was not quite as tall as Adam. Her head reached a little above his shoulders. She, too, was noble, perfect in symmetry, and very beautiful.

This chapter is based on Genesis 1.

Although God had made everything in the perfection of beauty, and the earth seemed to lack nothing to make Adam and Eve happy, yet God expressed His great love to them by planting a garden especially for them.

They would spend a portion of their time in the pleasant work of tending the garden, and a portion visiting with angels, listening to their instruction, and in happy reflection. Their labor was not tiring but enjoyable and invigorating. This beautiful garden was to be their home.

In this garden the Lord placed trees of every kind for usefulness and beauty. There were trees heavy with luxuriant fruit, rich in fragrance, beautiful to the eye, and pleasant to the taste, which God designed to be food for the holy pair. There were the lovely vines growing upright, laden with their burden of fruit. It was the happy work of Adam and Eve to form beautiful shady arches from the branches of the vine and train them, forming dwellings of nature's beautiful, living trees and foliage, bearing their fragrant fruit.

The earth was wrapped in beautiful living green, while thousands of fragrant flowers of every variety and color sprang up around Adam and Eve in rich profusion. Everything was tastefully and gloriously arranged. In the middle of the garden stood the tree of life, its glory greater than all other trees. Its fruit would keep them alive forever. The leaves contained healing properties.

Adam and Eve in Eden—The holy pair were very happy in Eden. God gave them unlimited control over every living thing. The lion and the lamb played peacefully and harmlessly around them or slept at their feet. Birds of every color and kind of plumage flitted among the trees and flowers and around Adam and Eve, while their mellow-toned music echoed among the trees in sweet harmony as they sang the praises of their Creator.

Adam and Eve were charmed with the beauties of their Eden home. They were delighted with the little songbirds around them, wearing their bright yet graceful plumage, and warbling out their happy, cheerful music. The holy pair united with them and raised their voices in harmonious songs of love, praise, and adoration to the Father and His Son for the evidences of love that surrounded them. They recognized the order and harmony of creation, which demonstrated wisdom and knowledge that were infinite.

They were always discovering some new beauty and additional glory of their Eden home, which filled their hearts with deeper love and brought from their lips expressions of gratitude and reverence to their Creator.

Chapter 3

The Tragedy

In the middle of the garden, near the tree of life, stood the tree of knowledge of good and evil. God had designed this tree specifically for them to give evidence of their obedience, faith, and love to Him. The Lord commanded our first parents not to eat from this tree, lest they die. He told them that they could eat freely from all the trees in the garden except one, but if they ate from that tree, they would surely die.

When God placed Adam and Eve in the beautiful garden, they had everything that they could desire for their happiness. But in His all-wise plans, God chose to test their loyalty before making them eternally secure. They would have His favor, and He would talk with them and they with Him. Yet He did not place evil out of their reach. Satan was allowed to tempt them. If they endured the test, they would be in the favor of God and the heavenly angels forever.

Satan was amazed at his new condition. His happiness was gone. He looked at the angels who, like him, were once so happy, but who had been expelled from heaven with him. Among them there was conflict, disagreement, and bitter accusations. Before their rebellion these things had been unknown in heaven. Satan now saw the terrible results of his rebellion.

If he could again be like he was when he was pure, true, and loyal, gladly would he have yielded up the claims of his authority. But he was lost! His groundless, willful rebellion had placed him beyond redemption!

And this was not all. He had led others to rebellion and the same lost condition with himself—angels, who had never thought to question the will of Heaven or to refuse obedience

This chapter is based on Genesis 2:15-17 and Genesis 3.

to the law of God till he had put it into their minds. Now they were in turmoil from disappointed hopes. Instead of greater good, they were experiencing the sad results of disobeying and disregarding God's law.

Satan Considers His Course—Satan trembled as he viewed his work. Alone, he thought about the past, the present, and his future plans. In his rebellion, he had had no reason for his course, and he had hopelessly ruined not only himself but the vast array of angels also, who would still have been happy in heaven if he had remained true. The law of God could condemn, but it could not pardon.

This great change of position had not increased his love for God or for His wise and just law. When Satan became fully convinced that there was no possibility of his being reinstated in God's favor, he revealed his evil intent with increased hatred and fiery passion.

God knew that such determined rebellion would not remain inactive. Satan would invent ways to annoy the heavenly angels and show contempt for His authority. Since he was not allowed within the gates of heaven, he would wait just at the entrance, to taunt the angels and to try to argue with them as they went in and out. He would seek to destroy the happiness of Adam and Eve. He would make every effort to stir them to rebellion, knowing that this would cause grief in heaven.

The Plot Against the Human Family—Satan told his followers about his plans to pull the noble Adam and his companion Eve away from God. If he could in any way trick them into disobedience, God would make some provision for them to be pardoned, and then he and all the fallen angels would be able to lay claim to a share of God's mercy with them.

If this failed, they could unite with Adam and Eve, because once they had transgressed the law of God, they would be subjects of God's wrath, too, like Satan and his angels. This transgression would place them, too, in a state of rebellion, like Satan and his angels, who could then unite with Adam and Eve, take possession of Eden, and hold it as their home. And if they could gain access to the tree of life in the middle of the garden, their strength, they thought, would be equal to that of the holy angels, and even God Himself could not expel them.

Adam and Eve Warned—God assembled the angels to take action to prevent the threatened evil. It was decided in heaven's council that angels would visit Eden and warn Adam that he was in danger from the enemy.

The angels gave Adam and Eve the sad history of Satan's rebellion and fall. They then distinctly informed them that the tree of knowledge was placed in the garden as a way for them to pledge their obedience and love to God. The holy angels could only keep their high and happy state on condition of obedience, and their situation was similar. They could obey the law of God and be inexpressibly happy, or disobey and lose their high position and be plunged into hopeless despair.

Angels told Adam and Eve that the most exalted angel, next in rank to Christ, refused to obey the law that God had established to govern heavenly beings. This rebellion, they said, had caused war in heaven, which resulted in the rebellious ones being expelled, and every angel who had united with this leader in questioning the authority of the great Jehovah had been driven out of heaven. This fallen angel was now an enemy to everything that God and His Son held dear.

They told them that Satan meant to do them harm, and it was necessary for them to be watchful, because they might come in contact with this fallen enemy. He could not harm them, though, while they obeyed God's command, because, if necessary, every angel from heaven would come to their help rather than allow him to harm them in any way. But if they disobeyed the command of God, then Satan would have power to annoy, perplex, and trouble them from that time on. If they remained firm against the first hints of evil from Satan, they were as secure as the heavenly angels.

But if they yielded to the tempter, the same God who did

not spare the exalted angels would not spare them. They must suffer the penalty for their transgression, for the law of God was as sacred as Himself, and He required wholehearted obedience from all in heaven and on earth.

The angels warned Eve not to separate from her husband in her occupations in the garden, because she might come in contact with this fallen enemy. If they were separated from each other, they would be in greater danger than if both were together.

Adam and Eve assured the angels that they would never disobey the express command of God. Rather, it was their highest pleasure to do His will.

TEMPTATION AND FALL

Satan took the form of a serpent and entered Eden. He positioned himself in the tree of knowledge and began leisurely eating of the fruit.

Unconsciously at first, Eve separated from her husband as she tended the garden. When she became aware of what had happened, she felt that there might be danger, but again she thought that she was safe, even if she did not remain close by the side of her husband. She had wisdom and strength to know if evil came, and to meet it. The angels had cautioned her not to do this. Eve found herself gazing at the fruit of the forbidden tree with a mixture of curiosity and admiration.

She saw that it was very lovely, and reasoned with herself about why God had so strictly prohibited them from eating it. Now was Satan's opportunity. He spoke to her as though he were able to read her thoughts: "Has God indeed said, 'You shall not eat of every tree of the garden'?" With soft and pleasant words, and with a musical voice, he addressed the amazed Eve. She was startled to hear a serpent speak, for she knew that God had not given the power of speech to the serpent.

Eve's curiosity was aroused. Instead of quickly leaving the spot, she listened to hear a serpent talk. It did not occur to her mind that this might be that fallen enemy, using the serpent as a medium. It was Satan who spoke, not the serpent. Eve was charmed, flattered, infatuated. If she had met a commanding personage, with a form like the angels and resembling them, she would have been on her guard.

That strange voice should have driven her to her husband's side to ask him why someone else should speak to her so freely. But she entered into a controversy with the serpent. She answered his question: "We may eat the fruit of the trees of the garden; but of the fruit of the tree which is in the midst of the garden, God has said, 'You shall not eat it, nor shall you touch it, lest you die.' " The serpent answered, "You will not surely die. For God knows that in the day you eat of it your eyes will be opened, and you will be like God, knowing good and evil."

Satan wanted them to think that by eating from the forbidden tree they would receive a new and more noble kind of knowledge than they already had. This has been his special work, with great success, ever since his fall—to lead people to pry into the secrets of the Almighty and not to be satisfied with what God has revealed, and not to be careful to obey what He has commanded. He wants to lead them to disobey God's commands and then make them believe that they are entering a wonderful field of knowledge. This is purely supposition, and it is a miserable deception.

They fail to understand what God *has* revealed, and they disregard His explicit commandments and aspire after wisdom independent of God, seeking to understand what He has chosen to withhold from mortals. They are elated with their ideas of progress and charmed with their own empty philosophy, but they grope in midnight darkness when it comes to true knowledge.

It was not God's will that this sinless pair should have any knowledge of evil. He had freely given them the good but withheld the evil. Eve thought the words of the serpent were wise, and she accepted his broad assertion, "You will not surely die. For God knows that in the day you eat of it your eyes will be opened, and you will be like God, knowing good and evil." This was making God a liar. Satan boldly implied that God had deceived them to keep them from achieving knowledge that would make them equal with Himself. God said, If you eat you will surely die. The serpent said, If you eat, "you will not surely die."

The tempter assured Eve that as soon as she ate the fruit she would receive a new and superior knowledge that would make her equal with God. He called her attention to himself. He said that the reason he had gained the power of speech was that he had eaten the fruit of the tree forbidden to them. He hinted that God would not carry out His word. It was merely a threat to intimidate them and keep them from great good. He also told them that they could not die. Hadn't they eaten from the tree of life which perpetuates immortality? He said that God was deceiving them to keep them from a higher state of being and a more exalted happiness.

The tempter plucked the fruit and passed it to Eve. She took it in her hand. Now, said the tempter, you were prohibited from even touching it lest you die. He told her that she would realize no more sense of evil and death in eating than she had in touching or handling the fruit. Eve was emboldened because she had not felt the immediate signs of God's displeasure. She thought the words of the tempter must be all wise and correct. She ate, and she was delighted with the fruit. It seemed delicious to her taste, and she imagined that she felt in herself the wonderful effects of the fruit.

Eve Becomes a Tempter—She then plucked some of the fruit for herself and ate it, imagining that she felt the invigorating power of a new and higher existence from the exhilarating influence of the forbidden fruit. She was in a strange and unnatural excitement as she went to find her husband with her hands filled with the forbidden fruit. She told him the wise things the serpent had said, and she wanted to take him immediately to the tree of knowledge. She told him she had eaten some of its fruit, and instead of feeling any sense of death, she experienced a pleasing, exhilarating influence. As soon as Eve had disobeyed, she became a powerful medium through which Satan could bring about the fall of her husband.

Adam understood very well that his companion had disobeyed the only prohibition that God had given them to test their faithfulness and love. Eve reasoned that the serpent said they would not surely die, and his words must be true, for she felt no signs of God's displeasure, but a pleasant influence, as she imagined the angels felt.

Adam regretted that Eve had left his side, but now the deed was done. He must be separated from the one whose companionship he had loved so well. How could he let that happen? His love for Eve was strong. And in utter discouragement he decided to share her fate. He reasoned that Eve was a part of himself, and if she must die, he would die with her, for he could not bear the thought of separation from her.

He lacked faith in his merciful and kind Creator. He did not think that God, who had formed him out of the dust of the ground into a living, beautiful being, and had created Eve to be his companion, could fill her place. After all, might not the words of this wise serpent be correct? Eve was standing before him, just as lovely and beautiful and apparently as innocent as before she had disobeyed. She expressed greater, higher love for him than before her disobedience, claiming that this resulted from her eating the fruit. He saw no signs of death in her.

He decided to take his chances. He grabbed the fruit and quickly ate it, and like Eve, he did not feel its ill effects immediately.

Man's Freedom of Choice—God instructed our first parents regarding the tree of knowledge, and they were fully informed about the fall of Satan and the danger of listening to his suggestions. God did not deprive them of the power to eat the forbidden fruit. He left them as free moral agents to believe His word, obey His commandments, and live, or to believe the tempter, disobey, and perish.

The sweet love and peace and happy contented bliss seemed removed from them, and in its place a lack of something came over them that they had never experienced before. Then for the first time they turned their attention to the external. They had not been clothed but were draped in light as the heavenly angels were. This light that had enshrouded them was now gone. To relieve their sense of lack and the nakedness they felt, they looked for some kind of covering for their bodies, for how could they meet the eye of God and angels unclothed?

Satan was overjoyed with his success. He had now tempted the woman to distrust God, to question His wisdom, and to try to penetrate His all-wise plans. And through her he had also overthrown Adam, who, because of his love for Eve, disobeyed the command of God and fell with her.

The Lord visited Adam and Eve and told them the result of their disobedience. As they heard God's majestic approach, they tried to hide themselves from the gaze of Him whom they had delighted to meet while they were in their innocence and holiness. "Then the Lord God called to Adam and said to him, 'Where are you?' So he said, 'I heard Your voice in the garden, and I was afraid because I was naked; and I hid myself.' And He said, 'Who told you that you were naked? Have you eaten from the tree of which I commanded you that you should not eat?' "

The Lord asked this question, not because He needed information, but for the conviction of the guilty pair. How did you become ashamed and fearful? Adam admitted his transgression, not because he repented for his great disobedience, but to blame his sin on God. "The woman whom You gave to be with me, she gave me of the tree, and I ate." God then addressed the woman: "What is this you have done?" Eve answered, "The serpent deceived me, and I ate."

The Curse—The Lord then spoke to the serpent: "Because you have done this, you are cursed more than all cattle, and more than every beast of the field; on your belly you shall go, and you shall eat dust all the days of your life." As the serpent had been exalted above the beasts of the field, he would be degraded beneath them all and be detested by people, because he was the medium through which Satan acted. "Then to Adam He said, 'Because you have heeded the voice of your wife, and have eaten from the tree of which I commanded you, saying, "You shall not eat of it": Cursed is the ground for your sake; in toil you shall eat of it all the days of your life. Both thorns and thistles it shall bring forth for you, and you shall eat the herb of the field. In the sweat of your face you shall eat bread till you return to the ground.' "

God cursed the ground because of their sin in eating from the tree of knowledge, and declared, "In toil you shall eat of it all the days of your life." He had allotted them the good and withheld the evil. Now He declares that they shall eat of it, that is, they would be acquainted with evil all the days of their life.

From that time forward, the human race would be afflicted by Satan's temptations. Adam was assigned a life of perpetual toil and anxiety instead of the happy, cheerful labor he had enjoyed up to then. They would experience disappointment, grief, and pain, and finally come to dissolution. They were made of the dust of the earth, and unto dust they would return.

They were informed that they would have to lose their Eden home. They had yielded to Satan's deception and believed the word of Satan, that God would lie. By their disobedience they had opened a way for Satan to gain access to them more easily, and it was not safe for them to remain in the Garden of Eden, in their state of sin to gain access to the tree of life and perpetuate a life of sin. They begged to be allowed to remain, although they admitted that they had lost all right to blissful Eden. They promised that in the future they would give God implicit obedience. They were told that in their fall from innocence to guilt they gained no strength, but great weakness. They had not kept their integrity while they were in a state of holy, happy innocence, and they would have far less strength to remain true and loyal in a state of conscious guilt. They were filled with the deepest anguish and remorse. They now realized that the penalty of sin was death.

Angels were commissioned immediately to guard the way to the tree of life. It was Satan's studied plan that Adam and Eve should disobey God, receive His frown, and then eat from the tree of life, so that they would perpetuate a life of sin. But holy angels were sent to block their way to the tree of life. Around these angels flashed beams of light on every side, which looked like glittering swords.

Chapter 4

The Solution

Sorrow filled heaven, as all realized that mankind was lost and the world that God had created was to be filled with mortals doomed to misery, sickness, and death, with no way of escape for the offender. The whole family of Adam must die.

Jesus then made known to the angelic host that a way of escape had been made for lost humanity. He told them that He had been pleading with His Father and had offered to give His life a ransom. He would take the sentence of death on Himself, that through Him human beings could find pardon. Through the merits of His blood, and obedience to the law of God, they could have the favor of God and be brought into the beautiful garden and eat from the fruit of the tree of life.

Jesus opened before them the plan of salvation. He told them that He would stand between the wrath of His Father and guilty humanity, that He would bear iniquity and scorn, and only a few would receive Him as the Son of God. Nearly everyone would hate and reject Him. He would leave all His glory in heaven, appear on earth as a man, humble Himself as a man, become acquainted by His own experience with the various temptations that would affect humanity, that He might know how to help those who would be tempted. Finally, after His mission as a teacher would be accomplished, He would be delivered into evil hands and endure almost every cruelty and suffering that Satan and his angels could inspire wicked men to inflict. He would die the cruelest of deaths, hung up between the heavens and the earth as a guilty sinner and suffering dreadful hours of agony, which even angels could not look upon, but would hide their faces from

This chapter is based on Genesis 3:15, 21-24.

the sight. Not merely agony of body would He suffer, but mental agony, to which bodily suffering could not compare. The weight of the sins of the whole world would be on Him. He told them He would die and rise again the third day, and would ascend to His Father to intercede for wayward, guilty human beings.

The One Possible Way of Salvation—The angels bowed down before Him. They offered their lives. Jesus said to them that by His death He would save many, that the life of an angel could not pay the debt. His life alone could His Father accept as a ransom for mankind. Afterward, those whom He redeemed would be with Him, and by His death He would ransom many and destroy Satan, who had the power of death. And His Father would give Him the kingdom and the greatness of the kingdom under the whole heaven, and He would possess it forever and ever. Satan and sinners would be destroyed, nevermore to disturb heaven or the purified new earth.

But He assigned the angels their work, to ascend and descend with strengthening help from glory to soothe the Son of God in His sufferings and minister to Him. Also, they were to guard and keep the subjects of grace from the evil angels and the darkness that Satan would constantly throw around them. It was impossible for God to alter or change His law to save lost, perishing sinners. Therefore, He allowed His beloved Son to die for their transgression.

Satan again rejoiced with his angels that by causing mankind's fall, he could pull down the Son of God from His exalted position. He told his angels that when Jesus would take the nature of fallen humanity, he could overpower Him and prevent the success of the plan of salvation.

In humility and inexpressible sadness Adam and Eve left the lovely garden where they had been so happy until they disobeyed the command of God. The atmosphere was changed. It was no longer unvarying, as it had been before their sin. God clothed them with coats of skins to protect them from the sense of chilliness and then of heat to which they were exposed.

God's Unchangeable Law—All heaven mourned because of Adam and Eve's disobedience and fall, which brought the wrath of God upon the whole human race. They were cut off from fellowship with God and were plunged in hopeless misery.

The law of Jehovah, the foundation of His government in heaven and on earth, was as sacred as God Himself, and for this reason God could not accept the life of an angel as a sacrifice for its transgression. His law is more important in His sight than the holy angels around His throne. The Father could not abolish or change one precept of His law to meet human beings in their fallen condition. But the Son of God, who with the Father had created them, could make an atonement for them that was acceptable to God, by giving His life as a sacrifice and bearing the wrath of His Father. Angels informed Adam that, as his sin had brought death and wretchedness, the sacrifice of Jesus Christ would bring life and immortality to light.

A View of the Future—God revealed future important events to Adam, from his expulsion from Eden to the Flood, and onward to the first advent of Christ on the earth. His love for Adam and his posterity would lead the Son of God to step down to take human nature, and so, through His own humiliation, elevate all who would believe on Him. Such a sacrifice was valuable enough to save the whole world. But only a few would accept the salvation brought to them through such a wonderful sacrifice. The majority would not comply with the conditions required of them to receive His great salvation. They would prefer sin and transgression of the law of God rather than repentance and obedience, relying by faith on the merits of the sacrifice offered. This sacrifice was of such infinite value as to make anyone who would accept it more precious than fine gold.

The Sacrificial Offering—When Adam made an offering for sin according to God's special directions, it was a most painful ceremony for him. His hand must take life, which God alone could give, and make an offering for sin. It was the first time he had witnessed death. As he looked at the bleeding victim, writhing in the agonies of death, he was to look forward by faith to the Son of God, whom the victim prefigured, who was to die as mankind's sacrifice.

This ceremonial offering, which God established, was to be a perpetual reminder to Adam of his guilt and also a repentant admission of his sin. This act of taking life gave Adam a deeper and more perfect sense of his transgression, which nothing less than the death of God's Son could wash away. He marveled at the infinite goodness and matchless love that would give such a ransom to save the guilty. As Adam was killing the innocent victim, it seemed to him that he was shedding the blood of the Son of God by his own hand. He knew that if he had remained true to God and to His holy law, there would have been no death of beast or human. Yet in the sacrificial offerings, which pointed to the great and perfect offering of God's own Son, there appeared a star of hope to illuminate the dark and terrible future, relieving it of its complete hopelessness and ruin.

In the beginning the head of each family was considered ruler and priest of his own household. Afterward, as the race multiplied on the earth, men of divine appointment performed this solemn worship of sacrifice for the people. The minds of sinners were to associate the blood of animals with the blood of the Son of God. The death of the victim was to testify to all that the penalty of sin was death. By the act of sacrifice, sinners acknowledged their guilt and showed their faith, looking forward to the great and perfect sacrifice of the Son of God, which the offering of animals prefigured. Without the atonement of the Son of God there could be no imparting of blessing or salvation from God to sinners. God was serious about upholding the honor of His law. The transgression of that law caused a fearful separation between

God and sinners. God allowed Adam in his innocence to have direct, free, and happy communion with his Maker. After his transgression, God would communicate to humanity through Christ and angels.

Chapter 5

The Liberation

God always has a people, even when they are far outnumbered by those who rebel against Him. For instance, only eight people—Noah and his family—got into the boat God instructed Noah to build as a refuge from the Flood. Enoch walked with God during largely godless times. God called Abraham to leave his native land and go to Canaan. His descendents, who became known as Israelites, lived there until a famine drove them to Egypt, where they were later enslaved. Here is the amazing story of how God liberated those who were living under Egyptian captivity more than a thousand years before Christ.

For many years the children of Israel had been in slavery to the Egyptians. Only a few families went down into Egypt, but they had become a large multitude. And being surrounded with idolatry, many of them had lost the knowledge of the true God and had forgotten His law. And they joined with the Egyptians in their worship of the sun, moon, and stars, and of animals and images, the work of men's hands.

Yet among the Hebrews there were some who preserved the knowledge of the true God, the Maker of the heavens and of the earth. The faithful ones were grieved, and in their distress they cried out to the Lord for deliverance from the Egyptian slavery, that He would bring them out of Egypt, where they could be rid of idol worship and the corrupting influences that surrounded them.

Although many of the Israelites had become corrupted by idolatry, the faithful stood firm. They had not concealed their faith, but openly acknowledged to the Egyptians that they served the only true and living God. They repeated the

This chapter is based on Exodus 5-15.

evidences of God's existence and power from creation onward. The Egyptians had an opportunity to become acquainted with the faith and the God of the Hebrews. They had tried to undermine the beliefs of the faithful worshipers of the true God, and they were annoyed because they had not succeeded, either by threats, the promise of rewards, or by cruel treatment.

The last two kings who had occupied the throne of Egypt had been tyrants who had cruelly treated the Hebrews. The elders of Israel had tried to encourage the sinking faith of the Israelites by reminding them of the promise God made to Abraham and the prophetic words of Joseph just before he died, foretelling their deliverance from Egypt. Some listened and believed. Others looked at their own sad condition and would not hope.

Pharaoh boasted that he would like to see their God deliver them from his hands. These words destroyed the hopes of many of the Israelites. The situation appeared to be very much as the king and his counselors had said. They knew that they were treated as slaves and that they must endure whatever degree of oppression their taskmasters and rulers might put upon them. Their male children had been hunted and killed. Their own lives were a burden, and they were believing in, and worshiping, the God of heaven.

Then they contrasted their condition with that of the Egyptians, who did not believe at all in a living God who had power to save or to destroy. Some of them worshiped idols, images of wood and stone, while others chose to worship the sun, moon, and stars. Yet they were prosperous and wealthy. And some of the Hebrews thought that if God was above all gods, He would not leave them like this as slaves to an idol-worshiping nation.

The time had come for God to answer the prayers of His oppressed people and to bring them out from Egypt with such mighty displays of His power that the Egyptians would have to acknowledge that the God of the Hebrews, whom they had despised, was above all gods. God would glorify His own name, so that other nations might hear of His power and tremble at His mighty acts, and so that His people, by witnessing His miraculous works, would fully turn from their idolatry to give Him pure worship.

In delivering Israel from Egypt, God plainly showed all the Egyptians His special mercy to His people. Since Pharaoh would not be convinced in any other way, God saw fit to execute His judgments on him, so that he might know by sad experience that God's power was superior to all others. He would give clear and undeniable proof to all nations of His divine power and justice, so that His name might be declared throughout all the earth. God intended that these exhibitions of power would strengthen the faith of His people, and that their descendents would faithfully worship Him alone who had performed such merciful wonders for them.

After Pharaoh's decree requiring the people to make bricks without straw, Moses declared to him that God, whom he pretended not to know, would compel him to yield to His claims and acknowledge His authority as supreme Ruler.

The Plagues—The miracles of turning the rod into a serpent and the river into blood did not move the hard heart of Pharaoh to let Israel go, but only increased his hatred of the Israelites. The work of his magicians led him to believe that Moses had performed these miracles by magic. However, when the plague of frogs was removed, he had abundant evidence that this was not the case. God could have caused them to disappear and return to dust in a moment, but He did not do this, so that after they would be removed, the king and the Egyptians could not say that it was the result of magic, like the work of the magicians. The frogs died, and then the people gathered them together into heaps. They could see the decaying frog bodies before them, which were corrupting the air. Here the king and all Egypt had evidences that their empty philosophy could not explain away, that this work was not magic but a judgment from the God of heaven.

The magicians could not produce the lice, which served as the next plague. The Lord would not allow them to make it even appear to themselves or to the Egyptian people that they could produce the plague of the lice. He would remove every excuse Pharaoh might have for unbelief. He compelled even the magicians themselves to say, "This is the finger of God."

Next came the plague of the swarms of flies. They were not such flies as harmlessly annoy us in some seasons of the year. Rather, the flies God brought on Egypt were large and venomous. Their sting was very painful to both humans and animals. God separated His people from the Egyptians and allowed no flies to appear throughout their areas.

The Lord then sent the plague of a disease on their cattle, and at the same time preserved the cattle of the Hebrews, so that not one of them died. Next came the plague of boils on both people and animals, and the magicians could not protect even themselves from it. The Lord then sent upon Egypt the plague of the hail mingled with fire, with lightnings and thunder. The time of each plague was given before it came, so that no one could say it had happened by chance. The Lord demonstrated to the Egyptians that the whole earth was under the command of the God of the Hebrews—that thunder, hail, and storm obey His voice. Pharaoh, the proud king who once inquired, "Who is the Lord, that I should obey His voice?" humbled himself and said, "I have sinned . . . : the Lord is righteous, and my people and I are wicked." He begged Moses to be his intercessor with God, to bring a stop to the terrific thunder and lightning.

The Lord next sent the dreadful plague of the locusts. The king chose to receive the plagues rather than to submit to God and let the Israelites leave Egypt. Without remorse he saw his whole kingdom under the miracle of these dreadful judgments. The Lord then sent darkness on Egypt. The people were not merely deprived of light, but the atmosphere was very oppressive, so that breathing was difficult. The Hebrews, however, had a pure atmosphere and light in their homes.

God brought one more dreadful plague upon Egypt, more severe than any before it. It was the king and the idol-worshiping priests who were opposed to the last the request of Moses. The people wanted the Hebrews to be allowed to leave Egypt. Moses warned Pharaoh and the people of Egypt, and also the Israelites, about the nature and effect of the last plague—the firstborn of every household would die. On that night, so terrible to the Egyptians and so glorious to the people of God, the solemn ordinance of the passover was instituted.

It was very hard for the Egyptian king and a proud and idol-worshiping people to accept the requirements of the God of heaven. Plague after plague came upon Egypt, and the king yielded no more than he was compelled to by the dreadful inflictions of God's wrath.

Every plague had come a little closer and more severe, and this one would be more dreadful than any before it. But the proud king was extremely angry, and he refused to humble himself. And when the Egyptians saw the great preparations being made among the Israelites for that dreadful night, they ridiculed the sign of blood sprinkled on the Israelite doorposts.

The Israelites had followed the directions God had given them, and while the angel of death was passing from house to house among the Egyptians, they were all ready for their journey and waiting for the rebellious king and his great men to tell them to go.

"And it came to pass at midnight that the Lord struck all the firstborn in the land of Egypt, from the firstborn of Pharaoh who sat on his throne to the firstborn of the captive who was in the dungeon, and all the firstborn of livestock. So Pharaoh rose in the night, he, all his servants, and all the Egyptians; and there was a great cry in Egypt, for there was not a house where there was not one dead.

"Then he called for Moses and Aaron by night, and said, 'Rise, go out from among my people, both you and the children of Israel. And go, serve the Lord as you have said. Also take your flocks and your herds, as you have said, and be gone; and bless me also.'

"And the Egyptians urged the people, that they might send them out of the land in haste. For they said, 'We shall all be dead.' So the people took their dough before it was leavened, having their kneading bowls bound up in their clothes on their shoulders. Now the children of Israel had done according to the word of Moses, and they had asked from the Egyptians articles of silver, articles of gold, and clothing. And the Lord had given the people favor in the sight of the Egyptians, so that they granted them what they requested. Thus they plundered the Egyptians."

The Lord revealed this to Abraham about four hundred years before it was fulfilled: "Then He said to Abram: 'Know certainly that your descendants will be strangers in a land that is not theirs, and will serve them, and they will afflict them four hundred years. And also the nation whom they serve I will judge; afterward they shall come out with great possessions.'" Genesis 15:13, 14.

"A mixed multitude went up with them also, and flocks and herds—a great deal of livestock." The children of Israel went out of Egypt with their possessions, which did not belong to Pharaoh, since they had never sold them to him. Jacob and his sons had taken their flocks and cattle with them into Egypt. The Israelites had become very great in number, and their flocks and herds had greatly increased. God had judged the Egyptians by sending the plagues on them, and made them hurry His people out of Egypt with all that they possessed.

The Pillar of Fire— "So they took their journey from Succoth and camped in Etham at the edge of the wilderness. And the Lord went before them by day in a pillar of cloud to lead the way, and by night in a pillar of fire to give them light, so as to go by day and night. He did not take away the pillar of cloud by day or the pillar of fire by night from before the people."

After the Hebrews had been gone from Egypt some days, the Egyptians told Pharaoh that they had fled and would never return to serve him again. And they were sorry that they had permitted them to leave Egypt. It was a very great loss for them to be deprived of the Israelites' services, and they regretted that they had consented to let them go. In spite of all they had suffered from the judgments of God, they were so hardened by their continual rebellion that they decided to go after the Israelites and bring them back to Egypt by force. The king took a very large army and six hundred chariots, and pursued after them, and overtook them while they were encamped by the sea.

"And when Pharaoh drew near, the children of Israel lifted their eyes, and behold, the Egyptians marched after them. So they were very afraid, and the children of Israel cried out to the Lord. Then they said to Moses, 'Because there were no graves in Egypt, have you taken us away to die in the wilderness? Why have you so dealt with us, to bring us up out of Egypt? Is this not the word that we told you in Egypt, saying, "Let us alone that we may serve the Egyptians"? For it would have been better for us to serve the Egyptians than that we should die in the wilderness.'

"And Moses said to the people, 'Do not be afraid. Stand still, and see the salvation of the Lord, which He will accomplish for you today. For the Egyptians whom you see today, you shall see again no more forever. The Lord will fight for you, and you shall hold your peace.' "

Deliverance at the Red Sea—"And the Lord said to Moses, 'Why do you cry to Me? Tell the children of Israel to go forward. But lift up your rod, and stretch out your hand over the sea and divide it. And the children of Israel shall go on dry ground through the midst of the sea.' " God wanted Moses to understand that He would work for His people—that their need would be His opportunity. When they had gone as far as they could, Moses must ask them still to go forward. He should use the rod God had given him to divide the waters.

" 'And I indeed will harden the hearts of the Egyptians, and they shall follow them. So I will gain honor over Pharaoh and over all his army, his chariots, and his horsemen. Then the Egyptians shall know that I am the Lord, when I have gained honor for Myself over Pharaoh, his chariots, and his horsemen.'

"And the Angel of God, who went before the camp of Israel, moved and went behind them; and the pillar of cloud went from before them and stood behind them. So it came between the camp of the Egyptians and the camp of Israel. Thus it was a cloud and darkness to the one, and it gave light by night to the other, so that the one did not come near the other all that night."

The Egyptians could not see the Hebrews, because the cloud of thick darkness was in front of them—the cloud that was all light to the Israelites. In this way God displayed His power to test His people, whether they would trust in Him after he gave them such evidences of His care and love for them, and to rebuke their unbelief and complaining. "Then Moses stretched out his hand over the sea; and the Lord caused the sea to go back by a strong east wind all that night, and made the sea into dry land, and the waters were divided. So the children of Israel went into the midst of the sea on the dry ground, and the waters were a wall to them on their right hand and on their left." The waters rose up and stood on either side like congealed walls, while Israel walked on dry ground in the middle of the sea.

The Egyptian army was celebrating through that night that the Israelites were again in their power. They thought there was no possibility of escape, for in front of the Israelites stretched the Red Sea, and the large armies of Egypt were close behind them. In the morning, when they came up to the sea and looked, there was a dry path, the waters were divided, standing like a wall on either side, and the people of Israel were halfway through the sea, walking on dry land. The Egyptians waited a while to decide what to do next. They were disappointed and enraged that, when the Hebrews were almost in their power, and they were sure of capturing them, an unexpected way was opened for them in the sea. They decided to follow them.

"And the Egyptians pursued and went after them into the midst of the sea, all Pharaoh's horses, his chariots, and his horsemen.

"Now it came to pass, in the morning watch, that the Lord looked down upon the army of the Egyptians through the pillar of fire and cloud, and He troubled the army of the Egyptians. And He took off their chariot wheels, so that they drove them with difficulty; and the Egyptians said, 'Let us flee from the face of Israel, for the Lord fights for them against the Egyptians.' "

The Egyptians dared to venture in the path God had prepared for His people, and angels of God went through their army and removed their chariot wheels. They were plagued. Their progress was very slow, and they began to worry. They remembered the judgments that the God of the Hebrews had brought on them in Egypt to compel them to let Israel go, and they thought that God might deliver them all into the hands of the Israelites. They decided that God was fighting for the Israelites, and they were terribly afraid and were turning around to flee from them, when "the Lord said to Moses, 'Stretch out your hand over the sea, that the waters may come back upon the Egyptians, on their chariots, and on their horsemen.' And Moses stretched out his hand over the sea; and when the morning appeared, the sea returned to its full depth, while the Egyptians were fleeing into it. So the Lord overthrew the Egyptians in the midst of the sea. Then the waters returned and covered the chariots, the horsemen, and all the army of Pharaoh that came into the sea after them. Not so much as one of them remained. But the children of Israel had walked on dry land in the midst of the sea, and the waters were a wall to them on their right hand and on their left.

"So the Lord saved Israel that day out of the hand of the Egyptians, and Israel saw the Egyptians dead on the seashore. Thus Israel saw the great work which the Lord had done in Egypt; so the people feared the Lord, and believed the Lord and His servant Moses."

As the Hebrews witnessed the marvelous work of God in the destruction of the Egyptians, they united in an inspired song of lofty eloquence and grateful praise.

Chapter 6

The Code

THE TEN COMMANDMENTS

God's Law Proclaimed at Mount Sinai—After the Lord had given the people of Israel such evidences of His power, He told them who He was: "I am the Lord your God, who brought you out of the land of Egypt, out of the house of bondage." The same God who revealed His power among the Egyptians now spoke His law:

"You shall have no other gods before Me.

"You shall not make for yourself a carved image—any likeness of anything that is in heaven above, or that is in the earth beneath, or that is in the water under the earth; you shall not bow down to them nor serve them. For I, the Lord your God, am a jealous God, visiting the iniquity of the fathers upon the children to the third and fourth generations of those who hate Me, but showing mercy to thousands, to those who love Me and keep My commandments.

"You shall not take the name of the Lord your God in vain, for the Lord will not hold him guiltless who takes His name in vain.

"Remember the Sabbath day, to keep it holy. Six days you shall labor and do all your work, but the seventh day is the Sabbath of the Lord your God. In it you shall do no work: you, nor your son, nor your daughter, nor your male servant, nor your female servant, nor your cattle, nor your stranger who is within your gates. For in six days the Lord made the heavens and the earth, the sea, and all that is in them, and rested the seventh day. Therefore the Lord blessed the Sabbath day and hallowed it.

This chapter is based on Exodus 19, 20, 25-40.

"Honor your father and your mother, that your days may be long upon the land which the Lord your God is giving you.

"You shall not murder.

"You shall not commit adultery.

"You shall not steal.

"You shall not bear false witness against your neighbor.

"You shall not covet your neighbor's house; you shall not covet your neighbor's wife, nor his male servant, nor his female servant, nor his ox, nor his donkey, nor anything that is your neighbor's."

The first and second commandments that Jehovah spoke are against idolatry, because worshiping idols would lead people to great lengths in sin and rebellion, and result in offering human sacrifices. God wants to guard against the least approach to such abominations. The first four commandments were given to show people their duty to God. The fourth is the connecting link between the great God and humanity. The Sabbath especially was given for the benefit of mankind and for the honor of God. The last six commandments show our duty to one another.

The Sabbath was to be a sign between God and His people forever. In this way it was to be a sign—all who would observe the Sabbath would show by doing so that they were worshipers of the living God, the creator of the heavens and the earth. The Sabbath was to be a sign between God and His people as long as He would have a people upon the earth to serve Him.

"Now all the people witnessed the thunderings, the lightning flashes, the sound of the trumpet, and the mountain smoking; and when the people saw it, they trembled and stood afar off. Then they said to Moses, 'You speak with us, and we will hear; but let not God speak with us, lest we die.'

"And Moses said to the people, 'Do not fear; for God has come to test you, and that His fear may be before you, so that you may not sin.' So the people stood afar off, but Moses drew near the thick darkness where God was.

"Then the Lord said to Moses, 'Thus you shall say to the children of Israel: "You have seen that I have talked with you from heaven." ' " The majestic presence of God at Sinai, and the commotions in the earth that His presence brought, the fearful thunderings and lightnings that accompanied this visitation of God, so impressed the minds of the people with fear and reverence for His sacred majesty that they drew back instinctively from the awesome presence of God, afraid that they would not be able to endure His terrible glory.

The Peril of Idol Worship—Again, God wanted to guard the Israelites from idolatry. He said to them, "You shall not make anything to be with Me—gods of silver or gods of gold you shall not make for yourselves." They were in danger of imitating the example of the Egyptians, making for themselves images to represent God.

God wanted His people to understand that He alone should be the object of their worship. When they would overcome the idol-worshiping nations around them, they were not to preserve any of the images of their worship, but destroy them completely. Many of these heathen gods were very costly and of beautiful workmanship, which might tempt those who had witnessed idol worship, so common in Egypt, even to regard these senseless objects with some degree of reverence. The Lord wanted His people to know that it was because of the idolatry of these nations, which had led them to every degree of wickedness, that He would use the Israelites as His instruments to punish them and destroy their gods.

After Moses had received the judgments from the Lord and had written them for the people, as well as the promises on condition of obedience, the Lord said to him, " 'Come up to the Lord, you and Aaron, Nadab and Abihu, and seventy of the elders of Israel, and worship from afar. And Moses alone shall come near the Lord, but they shall not come near; nor shall the people go up with him.'

"So Moses came and told the people all the words of the Lord and all the judgments. And all the people answered with one voice and said, 'All the words which the Lord has said we will do.' " Exodus 24:1-3.

Moses had written, not the Ten Commandments, but the judgments that God wanted them to observe and the promises conditional on their obedience to Him. He read this to the people, and they pledged themselves to obey all the words that the Lord had said. Moses then wrote their solemn pledge in a book and offered a sacrifice to God for the people. "Then he took the Book of the Covenant and read in the hearing of the people. And they said, 'All that the Lord has said we will do, and be obedient.' And Moses took the blood, sprinkled it on the people, and said, 'This is the blood of the covenant which the Lord has made with you according to all these words.' " The people repeated their solemn pledge to the Lord to do all that He had said and to be obedient. Exodus 24:7, 8.

God's Eternal Law—The law of God existed before human beings were created. The angels were governed by it. Satan fell because he transgressed the principles of God's government. After God created Adam and Eve, He made known to them His law. It was not written yet, but Jehovah taught it to them.

In Eden God instituted the Sabbath of the fourth commandment. After God had made the world and created mankind on the earth, He made the Sabbath for them. After Adam's sin and fall nothing was removed from the law of God. The principles of the Ten Commandments existed before the fall and were suitable for a holy order of beings. After the fall the principles of those commandments were not changed, but God gave additional laws to meet human beings in their fallen condition.

God established a system requiring sacrificing animals, to keep before fallen humanity the truth that the serpent made Eve disbelieve: that the penalty of disobedience is death. The transgression of God's law made it necessary for Christ to die as a sacrifice, and so to make a way possible for sinners to escape the penalty and yet preserve the honor of God's law. The system of sacrifices was to teach sinners humility, in view of their fallen condition, and lead them to repentance and to trust in God alone, through the promised Redeemer, for pardon for past transgression of His law. If there had been no transgression of God's law, there never would have been death, and there would have been no need for additional laws to address mankind's fallen condition.

Adam taught his descendants the law of God, which was handed down to the faithful through successive generations. The continual violation of God's law called for a flood of water on the earth. Noah and his family preserved the law, and for their right-doing they were saved in the ark by a miracle of God. Noah taught his descendants the Ten Commandments. From Adam onward, the Lord preserved a people for Himself, in whose hearts was His law. He says of Abraham, He "obeyed My voice and kept My charge, My commandments, My statutes, and My laws." Genesis 26:5.

The Lord appeared to Abraham and said to him:

"I am Almighty God; walk before Me and be blameless. And I will make My covenant between Me and you, and will multiply you exceedingly." Genesis 17:1, 2. "And I will establish My covenant between Me and you and your descendants after you in their generations, for an everlasting covenant, to be God to you and your descendants after you." Genesis 17:7.

He then required of Abraham and his descendants circumcision, which was a circle cut in the flesh, as a token that God had cut them out and separated them from all nations as His distinct treasure. By this sign they solemnly pledged not to intermarry with other nations, for by so doing they would lose their reverence for God and His holy law and would become like the idol-worshiping nations around them.

By the act of circumcision, they solemnly agreed to fulfill from their side the conditions of the covenant made with Abraham, to be separate from all nations and to be perfect. If the descendants of Abraham had kept separate from other nations, they would not have been lured into idolatry. By keeping separate from other nations, they would have removed a great temptation to engage in those nations' sinful practices and rebel against God. To a great degree, they lost their distinct, holy character by mingling with the nations around them. To punish them, the Lord brought a famine on their land, which compelled them to go down into Egypt to preserve their lives. But because of His covenant with Abraham, God did not abandon them while they were in Egypt. He allowed them to be oppressed by the Egyptians so that they might turn to Him in their distress, choose His righteous and merciful government, and obey His requirements.

There were only a few families that first went down into Egypt. These increased to a great number. Some were careful to instruct their children in the law of God, but many of the Israelites had witnessed so much idol worship that their ideas of God's law were confused. Those who honored God cried out to Him in anguish of spirit to break their slavery and bring them from the land of their captivity so that they could be free to serve Him. God heard their cries and raised up Moses as His instrument to deliver His people. After they had left Egypt and God had divided the waters of the Red Sea before them, the Lord tested them to see if they would trust in Him who had taken them as a nation out from another nation, by signs, trials, and wonders. But they failed to endure the test. They complained against God because of difficulties on the way, and they wanted to return again to Egypt.

Written in Tablets of Stone—To leave them without excuse, the Lord Himself condescended to come down on Mount Sinai, enshrouded in glory and surrounded by His angels. In a most sublime and impressive manner He made known to them His law of Ten Commandments. He did not entrust them to be taught by anyone else, not even His angels, but spoke His law Himself with an audible voice that all the people could hear. Even then, He did not entrust them to the short memory of a people who were prone to forget His requirements, but wrote them with His own holy finger on tablets of stone. He wanted to prevent all possibility that they would mingle any tradition with His holy laws or confuse His requirements with human practices.

He then came still closer to His people, who were so easily

led astray, and would not leave them with merely the ten commandments of the Decalogue. He commanded Moses to write judgments and laws by God's divine instruction, giving detailed directions regarding what He required them to do. In this way He guarded the ten precepts that He had engraved on the tablets of stone. He gave these specific directions and requirements to draw erring human beings to obey the moral law, which they are so prone to violate.

If mankind had kept the law of God, as given to Adam after his fall, preserved in the ark by Noah, and observed by Abraham, there would have been no need for the rite of circumcision. And if the descendants of Abraham had kept the covenant that circumcision represented, they would never have gone into idol worship or been permitted to go down into Egypt, and there would have been no need for God to proclaim His law from Sinai, engrave it on stone tablets, and guard it by definite directions in the judgments and statutes of Moses.

The Judgments and Statutes—Moses wrote these judgments and statutes that had come from the mouth of God while he was with Him on Mount Sinai. If the people of God had obeyed the principles of the Ten Commandments, they would not have needed the specific directions God gave to Moses about their duty to God and to one another, which he wrote in a book. The definite directions that the Lord gave to Moses regarding His people's duty to one another and to the stranger are the principles of the Ten Commandments, simplified and given in a definite manner, so that they need not be mistaken about them.

The Lord instructed Moses definitely concerning the ceremonial sacrifices that were to end at the death of Christ. The system of sacrifices foreshadowed the offering of Christ as a Lamb without blemish.

The Lord first established the system of sacrificial offerings with Adam after his fall, and Adam taught it to his descendants. This system was corrupted before the Flood, and by those who separated themselves from the faithful followers of God and built the tower of Babel. They sacrificed to gods of their own making instead of to the God of heaven. They offered sacrifices not because they had faith in the Redeemer to come but because they thought they should please their gods by offering a great many animal sacrifices on their polluted idol altars. Their superstition led them to great excesses. They taught the people that the more valuable the sacrifice, the greater pleasure would it give their idol gods and the greater would be the prosperity and riches of their nation. Therefore, human beings were often sacrificed to these senseless idols. To control the actions of the people, those nations had laws and regulations that were cruel in the extreme. Leaders whose hearts were not softened by grace were the ones making their laws. While they would ignore the most debasing crimes, a small offense would result in the most cruel punishment from those in authority.

Moses had this in mind when he said to Israel, "Surely I have taught you statutes and judgments, just as the Lord my God commanded me, that you should act according to them in the land which you go to possess. Therefore be careful to observe them; for this is your wisdom and your understanding in the sight of the peoples who will hear all these statutes, and say, 'Surely this great nation is a wise and understanding people.'

"For what great nation is there that has God so near to it, as the Lord our God is to us, for whatever reason we may call upon Him? And what great nation is there that has such statutes and righteous judgments as are in all this law which I set before you this day?" Deuteronomy 4:5-8.

THE EARTHLY SANCTUARY

The tabernacle was made according to the commandment of God. The Lord raised up craftsmen and qualified them with more than natural abilities to perform the most demanding work. Neither Moses nor those workmen were left to plan the form and workmanship of the building. God Himself devised the plan and gave it to Moses, with particular directions for its size and form and the materials to be used, and He specified every article of furniture that was to be in it. He showed Moses a miniature model of the heavenly sanctuary and commanded him to make everything according to the pattern shown him on the mountain. Moses wrote all the directions in a book and read them to the most influential people.

Then the Lord required the people to bring a free-will offering for making Him a sanctuary, so that He could dwell among them. "And all the congregation of the children of Israel departed from the presence of Moses. Then everyone came whose heart was stirred, and everyone whose spirit was willing, and they brought the Lord's offering for the work of the tabernacle of meeting, for all its service, and for the holy garments. They came, both men and women, as many as had a willing heart, and brought earrings and nose rings, rings and necklaces, all jewelry of gold, that is, every man who made an offering of gold to the Lord."

Great and expensive preparations were necessary. Rare and costly materials must be collected. But the Lord accepted only the free-will offerings. The first requirements in preparing a place for God were devotion to the work of God and sacrifice from the heart. And while the building of the sanctuary was going on and the people were bringing their offerings to Moses, and he was presenting them to the workmen, all the wise men who labored in the work examined the gifts and decided that the people had brought enough, and even more than they could use. And Moses announced throughout the camp, saying, " 'Let neither man nor woman do any more work for the offering of the sanctuary.' And the people were restrained from bringing."

Recorded for Later Generations—The repeated complaints of the Israelites and the punishments of God's wrath because of their transgressions are recorded in sacred history for the benefit of God's people who would afterward live on the earth. Even more so, they were to provide a warning to those who would live near the close of time. In addition, their acts of devotion and their energy and liberality in bringing their free-will offerings to Moses are recorded for the benefit of the people of God. Their cheerful preparing of material for the tabernacle is an example for all who truly love the worship of God. When preparing a building for Him to meet with them, those who prize the blessing of God's sacred presence should show greater interest and energy in the sacred work in proportion to how they value their heavenly blessings more highly than their earthly comforts. They should realize that they are preparing a house for God.

It is important that a building prepared expressly for God to meet with His people should be arranged with care—made comfortable, neat, and convenient, for they are to dedicate it to God and present it to Him, asking Him to abide in that house and make it sacred by His holy presence. They should give enough willingly to the Lord to accomplish the work liberally, and then the workmen should be able to say, Bring no more offerings.

According to the Pattern—After they completed building the tabernacle, Moses examined all the work, comparing it with the pattern and with directions he had received from God. He saw that every part of it agreed with the pattern, and he blessed the people.

God gave a pattern of the ark to Moses, with special directions how to make it. The ark was built to contain the tablets of stone on which God engraved the Ten Commandments with His own finger. It was shaped like a chest and was overlaid with pure gold inside and out. It was ornamented with crowns of gold around the top. The cover of this sacred chest was called the mercy seat, and it was made of solid gold. Attached on each end of the mercy seat was a cherub of pure, solid gold. Their faces were turned toward each other and were looking reverently downward toward the mercy seat. This represented all the heavenly angels looking with interest and reverence on the law of God deposited in the ark in the heavenly sanctuary. These cherubs had wings. One wing of each angel was stretched out above, while the other wing of each angel covered his body. The ark of the earthly sanctuary was patterned after the true ark in heaven. There, beside the heavenly ark, stand living angels, at either end of the ark, each with one wing overshadowing the mercy seat, and stretching out above it, while the other wings are folded over their forms in an expression of reverence and humility.

Moses was required to place the tablets of stone in the earthly ark. These were called the tablets of the testimony, and the ark was called the ark of the testimony, because they contained God's testimony in the Ten Commandments.

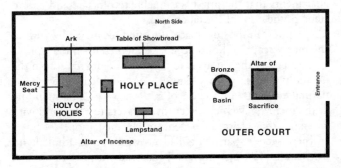

Two Apartments—The tabernacle was composed of two apartments, or rooms, separated by a curtain. All the furniture of the tabernacle was made of solid gold or was plated with gold. The curtains of the tabernacle were of various colors, most beautifully arranged, and in these curtains cherubim were woven, using threads of gold and silver. These were to represent the myriads of angels, who are connected with the work of the heavenly sanctuary and who are ministering angels to God's people on the earth.

Within the second curtain, or veil, was placed the ark of the testimony, and the beautiful, rich curtain was drawn in front of the sacred ark. This curtain did not reach to the top of the building. The glory of God, which was above the mercy seat, could be seen from both apartments, but in a much less degree from the first apartment.

Directly in front of the ark, but separated from it by the curtain, was the golden altar of incense. The Lord Himself had kindled the fire on this altar, and it was sacredly cherished by feeding it with holy incense, which filled the sanctuary with its fragrant cloud day and night. Its fragrance extended for miles around the tabernacle. When the priest offered the incense before the Lord, he looked to the mercy seat. Although he could not see it, he knew it was there, and as the incense arose like a cloud, the glory of the Lord descended on the mercy seat and filled the most holy place and was visible in the holy place. The glory often so completely filled both apartments that the priest was unable to officiate and had to stand at the door of the tabernacle.

The priest in the holy place, directing his prayer by faith to the mercy seat that he could not see, represents the people of God directing their prayers to Christ at the mercy seat in the heavenly sanctuary. They cannot see their Mediator with the natural eye, but with the eye of faith they see Christ standing at the mercy seat. They direct their prayers to Him, and with assurance they claim the benefits of His mediation.

These sacred apartments had no windows to admit light. The candlestick, or lampstand, was made of purest gold and was kept burning night and day, giving light to both apartments. The light of the lamps on the candlestick reflected on the gold-plated boards at the sides of the building and on the sacred furniture and the beautifully colored curtains with cherubim woven with threads of gold and silver. The appearance was glorious beyond description. No language can describe the beauty, loveliness, and sacred glory which these apartments presented. The gold in the sanctuary reflected the colors of the curtains, which appeared like the different colors of the rainbow.

Only once a year could the high priest enter into the most holy place, after the most careful and solemn preparation. No mortal eye but that of the high priest could look upon the sacred grandeur of that apartment, because it was the special dwelling place of God's visible glory. The high priest always entered it with trembling, while the people waited in solemn silence for his return. Earnestly they asked God for His blessing. At the mercy seat God conversed with the high priest. If he remained an unusually long time in the most holy place, the people were often terrified, fearing that the glory of the Lord had killed him because of their sins or some sin of the priest. But when they heard the tinkling sound of the bells on his garments, they were greatly relieved. He then came out and blessed the people.

After the work of the tabernacle was finished, "the cloud covered the tabernacle of meeting, and the glory of the Lord filled the tabernacle. And Moses was not able to enter the tabernacle of meeting, because the cloud rested above it, and the glory of the Lord filled the tabernacle." For "the cloud of the Lord was above the tabernacle by day, and fire was over it by night, in the sight of all the house of Israel, throughout all their journeys."

The tabernacle was made to be taken apart and carried with them in all their journeying.

The Guiding Cloud—The Lord directed the Israelites in all their travels through the wilderness. When it was for the good of the people and the glory of God for them to pitch their tents in a certain place and stay there, God indicated His will to them by having the pillar of cloud rest low directly over the tabernacle. And there it remained until God wanted them to journey again. Then the cloud of glory was lifted up high above the tabernacle, and then they traveled on.

In all their journeyings they maintained perfect order. Every tribe carried a standard—a flag or banner—with the sign of their father's family on it, and every tribe was commanded to pitch their tents by their own standard. And when they traveled, the different tribes marched in order, every tribe under their own standard. When they rested from their journeyings, the tabernacle was erected, and then the different tribes pitched their tents in order, in just such a position as God commanded, around the tabernacle, at a distance from it.

When the people journeyed, the ark of the covenant was carried in front of them. "And the cloud of the Lord was above them by day when they went out from the camp.

"So it was, whenever the ark set out, that Moses said: 'Rise up, O Lord! Let Your enemies be scattered, and let those who hate You flee before You.' And when it rested, he said: 'Return, O Lord, to the many thousands of Israel.' "

Chapter 7

The Deliverer

The time came when Jesus was to take upon Himself human nature, humble Himself as a man, and experience the temptations of Satan.

He was born without worldly grandeur, in a stable and cradled in a manger. Yet His birth was honored far above that of any other human being. Angels from heaven informed the shepherds of Jesus' arrival, and light and glory from God accompanied their testimony. The heavenly host touched their harps and glorified God. Triumphantly they heralded the advent of the Son of God to a fallen world to accomplish the work of redemption, and by His death to bring peace, happiness, and everlasting life to mankind. God honored the advent of His Son. Angels worshiped Him.

The Baptism of Jesus—Some thirty years later, angels of God hovered over the scene of His baptism. The Holy Spirit descended in the form of a dove and rested on Him, and as the people stood greatly amazed, with their eyes fastened on Him, they heard the Father's voice from heaven, saying, "You are My beloved Son, in whom I am well pleased." Mark 1:11.

John was not certain that it was the Savior who came to be baptized by him in the Jordan River. But God had promised him a sign by which he would know the Lamb of God. John recognized that sign when the heavenly dove rested on Jesus and the glory of God shone around Him. John reached out his hand, pointing to Jesus, and with a loud voice cried out, "Behold! The Lamb of God who takes away the sin of the world!" John 1:29.

The Ministry of John—John informed his disciples that

Jesus was the promised Messiah, the Savior of the world. As John's work was closing, he taught his disciples to look to Jesus and follow Him as the Great Teacher. John's life was sorrowful and self-denying. He announced the first advent of Christ but was not permitted to witness His miracles and enjoy the power that He manifested. When Jesus established Himself as a teacher, John knew that he himself must die. His voice was seldom heard, except in the wilderness. His life was lonely. He did not cling to his father's family, to enjoy their society, but left them in order to fulfill his mission. Crowds of people left the busy cities and villages, flocking to the wilderness to hear the words of the wonderful prophet. John went to the heart of the people's problem. He reproved sin, fearless of consequences, and prepared the way for the Lamb of God.

Herod was stirred as he listened to the powerful, pointed testimonies of John, and with deep interest he inquired what he must do to become his disciple. John knew that Herod was about to marry his brother's wife while her husband was still living, and he faithfully told Herod that this was not lawful. Herod was unwilling to make any sacrifice. He married his brother's wife and, influenced by her, arrested John and put him in prison, intending, however, to release him. While John was confined there, through his disciples he heard of the mighty works of Jesus. He could not go to listen to His gracious words, but the disciples informed him and comforted him with what they had heard. Soon John was beheaded, through the influence of Herod's wife. The humblest disciples who followed Jesus, witnessed His miracles, and heard the comforting words he spoke, were greater than John the Baptist (see Matthew 11:11); that is, they were more exalted and honored, and had more pleasure in their lives.

John came in the spirit and power of Elijah to proclaim the first advent of Jesus. Luke 1:17. John represented those in the last days who would go out in the spirit and power of Elijah to proclaim the day of wrath and the second advent of Jesus.

The Temptation—After the baptism of Jesus in the Jordan,

He was led by the Spirit into the wilderness, to be tempted by the devil. The Holy Spirit had prepared Him for that special scene of fierce temptations. Forty days He was tempted by Satan, and in those days He ate nothing. Everything around Him was unpleasant, which human nature would want to avoid. He was with the wild beasts and the devil in a desolate, lonely place. The Son of God was pale and emaciated, through fasting and suffering. But His course was laid out for Him, and He must fulfill the work that He came to do.

Satan took advantage of the sufferings of the Son of God and prepared to harass Him with many temptations, hoping to win the victory over Him because He had humbled Himself as a man. Satan came with this temptation: "If You are the Son of God, command this stone to become bread." He tempted Jesus to condescend to give him proof that He was the Messiah, by exercising His divine power. Jesus mildly answered him, "It is written, 'Man shall not live by bread alone, but by every word of God.' " Luke 4:3, 4.

Satan wanted to dispute with Jesus concerning His being the Son of God. He referred to His weak, suffering condition and boastingly affirmed that he was stronger than Jesus. But God's testimony from heaven, "You are My beloved Son; in You I am well pleased" (Luke 3:22), was sufficient to sustain Jesus through all His sufferings. Christ had no obligation to convince Satan of His power or that He was the Savior of the world. Satan has ample evidence of the exalted position and authority of the Son of God. His unwillingness to yield to Christ's authority had shut him out of heaven.

To show his own power, Satan carried Jesus to Jerusalem and set Him on a pinnacle of the temple, and there he tempted Him to give evidence that He was the Son of God by throwing Himself down from that dizzy height. Satan came with the inspired words the Bible: "For it is written: 'He shall give His angels charge over you, to keep you,' and, 'In their hands they shall bear you up, lest you dash your foot against a stone.' " Jesus answered, "It has been said, 'You shall not tempt the Lord your God.' " Luke 4:10-12.

Satan wanted to make Jesus presume on the mercy of His Father and risk His life before He could fulfill His mission. He had hoped that the plan of salvation would fail, but the plan was laid too deep for Satan to overthrow or mar it.

Christ is the example for all Christians. When they are tempted or their rights are disputed, they should bear it patiently. They should not feel that they have a right to call on the Lord to display His power so that they may obtain a victory over their enemies, unless God can be directly honored and glorified by doing so. If Jesus had thrown Himself down from the pinnacle of the temple, it would not have glorified His Father, for no one would have witnessed the act but Satan and the angels of God. And it would have been tempting the Lord to display His power to His bitterest foe. It would have been condescending to the one whom Jesus came to conquer.

"Then the devil, taking Him up on a high mountain, showed Him all the kingdoms of the world in a moment of time. And the devil said to Him, 'All this authority I will give You, and their glory; for this has been delivered to me, and I give it to whomever I wish. Therefore, if You will worship before me, all will be Yours.'

"And Jesus answered and said to him, 'Get behind Me, Satan! For it is written, "You shall worship the Lord your God, and Him only you shall serve." ' " Luke 4:5-8.

Satan showed Jesus the kingdoms of the world in the most attractive light. If Jesus would worship him right there, he offered to give up his claims to the possessions of earth. If the plan of salvation were carried out and Jesus should die to redeem sinners, Satan knew that his own power would be limited and finally taken away, and that he would be destroyed. Therefore it was his studied plan, if possible, to prevent Jesus from completing the great work He had begun. If God's plan of redemption should fail, Satan would retain the kingdom that he then claimed. He flattered himself that then he would reign in opposition to the God of heaven.

The Tempter Rebuked—Satan was elated when Jesus laid

aside His power and glory and left heaven. He thought that this placed the Son of God in his power. The temptation took so easily with the holy pair in Eden that he hoped by his satanic power and cunning to overthrow even the Son of God, and so save his own life and kingdom. If he could tempt Jesus to stray from the will of His Father, he would achieve his goal. But Jesus met the tempter with the rebuke, "Get behind Me, Satan!" He was to bow only to His Father.

Satan claimed the kingdom of earth as his and suggested to Jesus that He could avoid all His sufferings, that He did not need to die to obtain the kingdoms of this world. If He just would worship him, He could have all the possessions of earth and the glory of reigning over them. But Jesus was unmoved. He knew that the time was to come when, at the cost of His own life, He would redeem the kingdom from Satan, and that, after a time, all in heaven and earth would submit to Him. He chose His life of suffering and His dreadful death as the way that His Father had appointed for Him to become a lawful heir to the kingdoms of earth and have them given into His hands as an everlasting possession. Satan also will be given into His hands to be destroyed by death, never again to annoy Jesus or His redeemed people in glory.

THE MINISTRY OF CHRIST

After Satan had ended his temptations, he left Jesus for a while. Angels prepared Him food in the wilderness and strengthened Him, and His Father's blessing rested on Him. Satan's fiercest temptations had failed, yet he looked forward to the time of Jesus' ministry, when at different times he would try his schemes against Him. He still hoped to defeat Him by stirring up those who would not receive Jesus to hate Him and try to destroy Him.

Satan and his angels were very busy during Christ's ministry, inspiring people with unbelief, hate, and scorn. Often when Jesus spoke some cutting truth, pointing out their sins, the people would become enraged. Satan and his angels urged them on to take the life of the Son of God. More than once they picked up stones to throw at Him, but angels guarded Him and took Him away from the angry mob to a place of safety. Again, as the plain truth came from His holy lips, the crowd laid hold of Him and led Him to the brow of a hill, intending to throw Him down. A dispute arose among them over what they should do with Him, when the angels again hid Him from the sight of the crowd, and He passed through the midst of them and went His way.

Satan still hoped that the great plan of salvation would fail. He exerted all his power to make the hearts of the people hard and their feelings bitter against Jesus. He hoped that so few would receive Him as the Son of God that He would consider His sufferings and sacrifice too great to make for so small a group. But if there had been only two who would have accepted Jesus as the Son of God and believed on Him for salvation, He would have carried out the plan.

Relieving the Suffering—Jesus began His work by breaking Satan's power over the suffering. He restored the sick to health, gave sight to the blind, and healed the lame, causing them to leap for joy and to glorify God. He restored health to those who had been ill, held in Satan's cruel power many years. With gracious words He comforted the weak, the trembling, and the desponding. The feeble, suffering ones whom Satan held in triumph, Jesus wrenched from his grasp, bringing them physical health and great joy and happiness. He raised the dead to life, and they glorified God for the mighty display of His power. He worked powerfully for all who believed on Him.

The life of Christ was filled with words and acts of kindness, sympathy, and love. He was always ready to listen to and relieve the problems of those who came to Him. The healed bodies of large numbers of people carried the evidence of His divine power. Yet after He had accomplished so much for them, many were ashamed of the humble yet mighty Preacher. Because the rulers did not believe on Him, the people were not willing to accept Jesus. He was a man of sorrows and acquainted with grief. They could not tolerate being governed by His sober, self-denying life. They wanted to enjoy the honor that the world bestows. Yet many followed the Son of God and listened to His instructions, feasting on the words that fell so graciously from His lips. His words were full of meaning, yet so plain that the weakest could understand them.

Ineffective Opposition—Satan and his angels blinded the eyes and darkened the understanding of the Jews, and stirred up the chief of the people and the rulers to take the Savior's life. The rulers sent others to bring Jesus to them, but as these came near where He was they were greatly amazed. They saw Him filled with sympathy and compassion as He witnessed human suffering. They heard Him in love and tenderness speak encouragingly to the weak and afflicted. They also heard Him, in a voice of authority, rebuke the power of Satan and command his captives to go free. They listened to His words of wisdom, and they were captivated. They could not arrest Him. They returned to the priests and elders without Jesus.

When asked, "Why have you not brought Him?" they told what they had seen of His miracles, and the holy words of wisdom, love, and knowledge that they had heard. They ended by saying, "No man ever spoke like this Man!" John 7:45, 46. The chief priests accused them of being also deceived, and some of the officers were ashamed that they had not taken Him into custody. The priests inquired scornfully if any of the rulers had believed on Him. Many of the magistrates and elders did believe on Jesus, but Satan kept them from admitting it. They feared the scorn of the people more than they feared God.

So far the scheming and hatred of Satan had not broken up the plan of salvation. The time was drawing near for Jesus to accomplish the purpose for which He had come into the world. Satan and his angels consulted together and decided to inspire Christ's own nation to cry eagerly for His blood and heap cruelty and scorn on Him. They hoped that Jesus would resent such treatment and fail to maintain His humility and meekness.

While Satan was laying his plans, Jesus was carefully opening to His disciples the sufferings through which He must pass—that He would be crucified and that He would rise again the third day. But their understanding seemed dull, and they could not comprehend what He told them.

The Transfiguration—The faith of the disciples was greatly strengthened at the transfiguration, when they were permitted to see Christ's glory and to hear the voice from heaven testifying to His divine character. (See Matthew 17:1-8.) God chose to give the followers of Jesus strong proof that He was the promised Messiah, so that in their bitter sorrow and disappointment at His crucifixion, they would not lose their faith entirely. At the transfiguration the Lord sent Moses and Elijah to talk with Jesus concerning His sufferings and death. Instead of choosing angels to converse with His Son, God chose those who had themselves experienced the trials of earth.

Elijah had walked with God. His work had been painful and trying, for through him the Lord had pointed out the sins of Israel. Elijah was a prophet of God, yet he had to flee from place to place to save his life. His own nation hunted him like a wild beast in order to destroy him. But God translated Elijah. Angels bore him in glory and triumph to heaven, without his tasting death.

Moses was greater than any who had lived before him. God had highly honored him. He had been privileged to talk with the Lord face to face, as a man speaks with a friend. He was permitted to see the bright light and excellent glory that enshrouds the Father. Through Moses the Lord delivered the Israelites from Egyptian slavery. Moses was a mediator for his people, often standing between them and the wrath of God. When the anger of the Lord was great against Israel for their unbelief, their complaining, and their deplorable sins, Moses' love for them was tested. God proposed to destroy them and to make a mighty nation from him. Moses showed his love for

Israel by his earnest pleading in their behalf. In his distress he prayed God to turn from His fierce anger and forgive Israel, or blot his name out of His book.

Moses passed through death, but Michael came down and gave him life before his body had experienced decay. Satan tried to hold the body, claiming it as his, but Michael resurrected Moses and took him to heaven. Satan railed bitterly against God, denouncing Him as unjust in permitting his prey to be taken from him. But Christ did not rebuke His adversary, though it was through Satan's temptation that the servant of God had fallen. He meekly referred him to His Father, saying, "The Lord rebuke you!" Jude 9.

Jesus had told His disciples that there were some standing with Him who would not taste of death till they saw the kingdom of God come with power. At the transfiguration this promise was fulfilled. The face of Jesus was changed there, shining like the sun. His clothing was white and glistening. Moses was there to represent those who will be raised from the dead at the second coming of Jesus. And Elijah, who was translated without seeing death, represented those who will be changed to immortality at Christ's return and will be translated to heaven without seeing death. With astonishment and fear the disciples saw the excellent majesty of Jesus and the cloud that overshadowed them, and they heard the voice of God in terrifying majesty, saying, "This is My beloved Son. Hear Him!"

Chapter 8

The Sacrifice

THE BETRAYAL OF CHRIST

Satan had deceived Judas and led him to think that he was one of Christ's true disciples, but his heart had always been carnal. He had seen the mighty works of Jesus, been with Him through His ministry, and had yielded to the overpowering evidence that He was the Messiah, but Judas was stingy and covetous. He loved money. He complained angrily about the costly ointment that Mary poured on Jesus.

Mary loved her Lord. He had forgiven her sins, which were many, and had raised from the dead her much-loved brother, and she felt that nothing was too valuable to bestow on Jesus. The more precious the ointment, the better she could express her gratitude to her Savior by devoting it to Him.

As an excuse for his greed, Judas urged that the ointment might have been sold and given to the poor. But it was not because he had any care for the poor. He was selfish, and he often took for his own use the funds entrusted to his care to be given to the poor. Judas had been careless about the comfort and even the needs of Jesus, and to excuse his covetousness he often referred to the poor. Mary's act of generosity was a most cutting rebuke of his covetous character. This prepared the way for Satan's temptation to find a ready reception in Judas's heart.

The priests and rulers of the Jews hated Jesus, but great crowds thronged to listen to His words of wisdom and to witness His mighty works. The people were stirred with the deepest interest and anxiously followed Jesus to hear the instructions of this wonderful Teacher. Many of the rulers believed on Him, but they did not dare confess their faith for fear of being put out of the synagogue. The priests and elders decided that something must be done to draw the attention of the people from Jesus. They feared that everyone would believe on Him. They could see no safety for themselves. They must either lose their position or put Jesus to death. And after they would put Him to death, there would still be those who were living monuments of His power.

Jesus had raised Lazarus from the dead, and they feared that if they were to kill Jesus, Lazarus would testify of His mighty power. The people were flocking to see the man who was raised from the dead, and the rulers determined to kill Lazarus also and put down the excitement. Then they would turn the people to human traditions and doctrines, to tithe mint and rue, and again have influence over them. They agreed to arrest Jesus when He was alone, because if they attempted to take Him in a crowd when the minds of the people were all interested in Him, they would be stoned.

Judas knew how anxious they were to get Jesus, and he offered to betray Him to the chief priests and elders for a few pieces of silver. His love of money led him to agree to betray his Lord into the hands of His bitterest enemies. Satan was working directly through Judas, and in the midst of the impressive scene of the last supper the traitor was making plans to betray his Master. Jesus sorrowfully told His disciples that all of them would be offended that night because of Him. But Peter ardently asserted that although all others might be offended because of Him, he would not be offended. Jesus said to Peter, "Satan has asked for you, that he may sift you as wheat. But I have prayed for you, that your faith should not fail; and when you have returned to Me, strengthen your brethren." Luke 22:31, 32.

In the Garden—Jesus was in the garden of Gethsemane with His disciples. In deep sorrow He asked them to watch and pray, so that they would not enter into temptation. He knew that their faith was to be tried and their hopes would be disappointed, and that they would need all the strength that they could obtain by earnest watching and fervent prayer.

With strong cries and weeping, Jesus prayed, "Father, if it is Your will, take this cup away from Me; nevertheless not My will, but Yours, be done." Luke 22:42. The Son of God prayed in agony. Great drops of blood gathered on His face and fell to the ground. Angels were hovering over the place, witnessing the scene, but only one was commissioned to go and strengthen the Son of God in His agony.

After Jesus had prayed He came to His disciples, but they were sleeping. In that dreadful hour He did not have the sympathy and prayers of even His disciples. Peter, who had been so zealous a short time before, was heavy with sleep. Jesus reminded him of his positive declarations and said to him, "What? Could you not watch with Me one hour?" Matthew 26:40. Three times the Son of God prayed in agony.

Judas Betrays Jesus—Then Judas appeared with his band of armed men. He approached His Master as usual, to greet Him. The armed group surrounded Jesus, but then He displayed His divine power, as He said, "Whom are you seeking?" "I am He." They fell backward to the ground. Jesus asked this question so that they could witness His power and have evidence that He could deliver Himself from their hands if He wished.

The disciples began to hope as they saw the crowd with their clubs and swords fall so quickly. As they arose and again surrounded the Son of God, Peter drew his sword and struck a servant of the high priest, cutting off an ear. Jesus ordered him to put the sword away, saying, "Do you think that I cannot now pray to My Father, and He will provide Me with more than twelve legions of angels?" Matthew 26:53. When He spoke these words, the faces of the angels were animated with hope. They wanted to surround their Commander then and there and disperse that angry mob. But again sadness settled over them, as Jesus added, "How then could the Scriptures be fulfilled, that it must happen thus?" Matthew 26:54. The hearts of the disciples also sank in despair and bitter disappointment as Jesus allowed Himself to be led away by His enemies.

The disciples feared for their own lives, and they all abandoned Him and ran away. Jesus was left alone in the hands of the murderous mob. Oh, what a triumph of Satan then! And what sadness and sorrow among the angels of God! Many companies of holy angels, each with a tall, commanding angel at their head, were sent to witness the scene. They were to record every insult and cruelty imposed upon the Son of God, and to register every pang of anguish that Jesus would suffer, for the very men who joined in this dreadful scene are to see it all again in lifelike display.

THE TRIAL OF CHRIST

Satan and his angels were busy in the judgment hall, destroying human feeling and sympathy. The very atmosphere was heavy and polluted by their influence. They inspired the chief priests and elders to insult and abuse Jesus in the most difficult way for human nature to bear. Satan hoped that such mockery and violence would draw some complaint or murmur from the Son of God, or that He would display His divine power and wrench Himself from the grasp of the mob, so that in this way the plan of salvation might at last fail.

Peter's Denial—Peter followed his Lord after His betrayal. He was anxious to see what would happen to Jesus. But when he was accused of being one of His disciples, fear for his own safety led him to declare that he did not know the Man. The disciples were known for the purity of their language, and Peter, to convince his accusers that he was not one of Christ's disciples, denied the charge the third time with cursing and swearing. Jesus, who was some distance away from Peter, turned a sorrowful, reproving gaze on him. Then the disciple remembered the words Jesus had spoken to him in the upper room, and also his own passionate assertion, "Even if all are made to stumble because of You, I will never be made to stumble." Matthew 26:33. He had denied his Lord, even with cursing and swearing, but that look of Jesus' melted Peter's heart and saved him. He wept bitterly and repented of his great sin, and was converted, and then he was prepared to strengthen his brethren.

In the Judgment Hall—The mob clamored for the blood of Jesus. The soldiers cruelly scourged Him, put an old purple kingly robe on Him, and encircled His sacred head with a crown of thorns. They put a reed into His hand and bowed to Him, mockingly greeting Him, "Hail, King of the Jews!" John 19:3. They then took the reed from His hand and struck Him on the head with it, causing the thorns to pierce His temples, sending the blood trickling down His face and beard.

Jesus knew that angels were witnessing the scene of His humiliation. The weakest angel could have delivered Jesus, causing that mocking crowd to fall powerless. Jesus knew that if He asked His Father, angels would instantly release Him. But it was necessary for Him to suffer the violence of wicked men, in order to carry out the plan of salvation.

Jesus stood meek and humble before the infuriated mob while they inflicted on Him the vilest abuse. They spat in His face— that face from which they will one day want to hide, which will give light to the city of God and will shine brighter than the sun. Christ did not so much as cast an angry look at the offenders. They covered His head with an old garment, blindfolding Him, and then struck Him in the face and demanded, "Prophesy! Who is the one who struck You?" Luke 22:64.

Some of the disciples had gained confidence to enter where Jesus was and witness His trial. They expected Him to show His divine power, deliver Himself from the hands of His enemies, and punish them for their cruelty toward Him. Their hopes would rise and fall as the different scenes unfolded. Sometimes they doubted, fearing that they had been deceived. But the voice they had heard at the mount of transfiguration, and the glory they had seen there, strengthened their faith that He was the Son of God. They called to mind the scenes they had witnessed, the miracles they had seen Jesus perform in healing the sick, opening the eyes of the blind, unstopping the deaf ears, rebuking and casting out devils, raising the dead to life, and even calming the wind and the sea.

They could not believe that He would die. They hoped that He would yet rise in power, and with His commanding voice disperse that bloodthirsty mob, as when He entered the temple and drove out the vendors and money-changers who were making the house of God a place of merchandise, when they ran from Him as if a company of armed soldiers was pursuing them. The disciples hoped that Jesus would display His power and convince all that He was the King of Israel.

Judas's Confession—Judas was filled with bitter remorse and shame at his treacherous act in betraying Jesus. And when he witnessed the abuse that the Savior endured, he was overcome. He had loved Jesus, but had loved money more. He had not thought that Jesus would allow Himself to be taken by the mob that he had led. He had expected Him to work a miracle and deliver Himself from them. But when he saw the infuriated crowd in the judgment hall, thirsting for blood, he deeply felt his guilt. While many were vehemently accusing Jesus, Judas rushed through the crowd, confessing that he had sinned in betraying innocent blood. He offered the priests the money they had paid him, and he begged them to release Jesus, declaring that He was entirely innocent.

For a short time, anger and confusion kept the priests silent. They did not want the people to know that they had hired one of the professed followers of Jesus to betray Him into their hands. They wanted to hide the fact that they had hunted Jesus like a thief and taken Him secretly. But the confession of Judas and his haggard, guilty appearance exposed the priests before the crowd, showing that it was hatred that had caused them to arrest Jesus. As Judas loudly declared that Jesus was innocent, the priests replied, "What is that to us? You see to it!" Matthew 27:4. They had Jesus in their power and were determined to carry out their plans. Judas, overwhelmed with anguish, threw the money that he now despised at the feet of those who had hired him, and, in anguish and horror, went and hanged himself.

Jesus had many sympathizers in the assembly around Him, and His answering nothing to the many questions put to Him amazed the crowd. Under all the mockery and violence of the mob, not a frown, not a troubled expression, rested on His features. He was dignified and composed. The spectators looked at Him with amazement. They compared His perfect form and firm, dignified bearing with the appearance of those who sat in judgment against Him, and they said to one another that He appeared more like a king than any of the rulers. He bore no signs of being a criminal. His eye was mild, clear, and undaunted, His forehead broad and high. Every feature was strongly marked with kindness and noble principle. His patience and self-restraint were so unlike an ordinary human that many trembled. Even Herod and Pilate were greatly troubled at His noble, Godlike bearing.

Jesus Before Pilate—From the first, Pilate was convinced that Jesus was no common man. He believed Him to be of excellent character and entirely innocent of the charges brought against Him. The angels who were witnessing the scene noticed the convictions of the Roman governor, and to save him from the awful act of delivering Christ to be crucified, an angel was sent to Pilate's wife, who gave her information through a dream that it was the Son of God in whose trial her husband was engaged, and that He was an innocent sufferer. She immediately sent a message to Pilate, stating that she had suffered many things in a dream because of Jesus and warning him to have nothing to do with that holy Man. The messenger, pushing hastily through the crowd, placed the letter in Pilate's hands. As he read, he trembled and turned pale, and immediately determined to have nothing to do with putting Christ to death. If the Jews wanted the blood of Jesus, he would not give his influence to it, but would work to deliver Him.

Sent to Herod—When Pilate heard that Herod was in Jerusalem, he was greatly relieved, for he hoped to free himself from all responsibility in the trial and condemnation of Jesus. Immediately he sent Him, with His accusers, to Herod. This ruler had become hardened in sin. The murder of John the Baptist had left on his conscience a stain from which he could not free himself. When he heard of Jesus and the mighty works done by Him, he feared and trembled, believing Him to be John the Baptist risen from the dead. When Pilate turned Jesus over to him, Herod considered the act an acknowledgment of his power, authority, and judgment. This had the effect of making friends of the two rulers, who before this had been enemies. Herod was pleased to see Jesus, expecting Him to work some mighty miracle for his satisfaction. But it was not the work of Jesus to gratify curiosity or to seek His own safety. He would exercise His divine, miraculous power for the salvation of others, but not in His own behalf.

Jesus answered nothing to the many questions Herod put to Him, nor did He reply to His enemies, who were vehemently accusing Him. Herod was enraged because Jesus did not appear to fear his power, and with his men of war he derided, mocked, and abused the Son of God. Yet he was astonished at the noble, Godlike appearance of Jesus when shamefully abused, and, afraid to condemn Him, he sent Him back to Pilate.

Satan and his angels were tempting Pilate and trying to lead him on to his own ruin. They suggested to him that if he did not take part in condemning Jesus, others would. The crowd was thirsting for His blood, and if Pilate did not deliver Him to be crucified, he would lose his power and worldly honor and would be denounced as a believer in the impostor. Through fear of losing his power and authority, Pilate consented to the death of Jesus. And even though he placed the blood of Jesus upon His accusers, and the mob received it, crying, "His blood be on us, and on our children" (Matthew 27:25), yet Pilate was not clear of responsibility; he was guilty of the blood of Christ. For his own selfish interest, his love of honor from the great men of earth, he delivered an innocent man to die. If Pilate had followed his own convictions, he would have had nothing to do with condemning Jesus.

The appearance and words of Jesus during His trial made a deep impression on the minds of many who were there. The result of this influence was apparent after His resurrection. Among those who were then added to the church, there were many whose conviction dated from the time of Jesus' trial.

Satan's rage was great as he saw that all the cruelty he had led the Jews to inflict on Jesus had not called forth from Him the slightest complaint. Although He had taken upon Himself human nature, He was sustained by a Godlike fortitude, and He did not depart in the least from the will of His Father.

THE CRUCIFIXION OF CHRIST

Christ, the precious Son of God, was led out and delivered to the people to be crucified. The disciples and believers from the surrounding region joined the crowd that followed Jesus to Calvary. The mother of Jesus was also there, supported by John, the beloved disciple. Her heart was filled with unutterable anguish, yet along with the disciples, she hoped that the painful scene would change, and Jesus would assert His power and appear before His enemies as the Son of God. Then again her mother heart would sink as she remembered words in which He had briefly referred to the things that were being enacted that day.

Jesus had scarcely passed the gate of Pilate's house when the cross that had been prepared for Barabbas was brought out and laid on His bruised and bleeding shoulders. Crosses were also placed upon the companions of Barabbas, who were to suffer death at the same time with Jesus. The Savior had carried His burden only a short distance when, from loss of blood and extreme weariness and pain, He fell fainting to the ground.

When Jesus revived, the cross was again placed on His shoulders, and He was forced forward. He staggered on for a few steps, bearing His heavy load, then fell to the ground like someone lifeless. He was at first pronounced to be dead, but finally he again revived. The priests and rulers felt no compassion for their suffering victim, but they saw that it was impossible for Him to carry the instrument of torture any farther. While they were considering what to do, Simon, a Cyrenian, coming from an opposite direction, met the crowd. At the instigation of the priests he was seized and compelled to carry the cross of Christ. The sons of Simon were disciples of Jesus, but he himself had never been connected with Him.

A large crowd followed the Savior to Calvary. Many were mocking and deriding, but some were weeping and recounting His praise. Those whom He had healed of various ailments and those He had raised from the dead earnestly declared His marvelous works and demanded to know what Jesus had done that He should be treated as a criminal. Only a few days before, they had accompanied Him with joyful hosannas and the waving of palm branches as He rode triumphantly to Jerusalem. But many who had then shouted His praise because it was popular to do so now swelled the cry of "Crucify Him! Crucify Him!"

Nailed to the Cross—When they arrived at the place of execution, the condemned were bound to the instruments of torture. While the two thieves wrestled in the hands of those who stretched them upon the cross, Jesus made no resistance. The mother of Jesus looked on with agonizing suspense, hoping that He would work a miracle to save Himself. She saw His hands stretched upon the cross—those dear hands that had always dispensed blessings and had reached out so many times to heal the suffering. And now the hammer and nails were brought, and as the spikes were driven through the tender flesh and fastened to the cross, the heart-stricken disciples bore away from the cruel scene the fainting form of the mother of Christ.

Jesus made not the slightest complaint. His face remained pale and serene, but great drops of sweat stood upon His brow. There was no pitying hand to wipe the death dew from His face, nor words of sympathy and unchanging loyalty to cheer His human heart. He was treading the winepress all alone; and of all the people there was none with Him. While the soldiers were doing their fearful work and He was enduring the most acute agony, Jesus prayed for His enemies: "Father, forgive them; for they do not know what they do." Luke 23:34. That prayer of Christ for His enemies embraced the world, taking in every sinner who would ever live, until the end of time.

After Jesus was nailed to the cross, it was lifted by several powerful men and thrust with great violence into the place prepared for it, causing the most excruciating agony to the Son of God. And now a terrible scene took place. Priests, rulers, and scribes forgot the dignity of their sacred offices and joined with the rabble in mocking and jeering the dying Son of God, saying, "If You are the King of the Jews, save Yourself." Luke 23:37. And some deridingly repeated among themselves, "He saved others; Himself He cannot save." Mark 15:31. The dignitaries of the temple, the hardened soldiers, the vile thief on the cross, and the base and cruel among the multitude—all united in their abuse of Christ.

The thieves who were crucified with Jesus suffered the same physical torture with Him: but one was only hardened and made desperate and defiant by his pain. He echoed the mocking of the priests and railed against Jesus, saying, "If You are the Christ, save Yourself and us." Luke 23:39. The other condemned man was not a hardened criminal. When he heard the sneering words of his companion in crime, he "rebuked him, saying, 'Do you not even fear God, seeing you are under the same condemnation? And we indeed justly, for we receive the due reward of our deeds; but this Man has done nothing wrong.'" Luke 23:40, 41. Then, as his heart went out to Christ, heavenly illumination flooded his mind. In Jesus, bruised, mocked, and hanging upon the cross, he saw his Redeemer, his only hope, and appealed to Him in humble faith: "'Lord, remember me when You come into Your kingdom.'"

"And Jesus said to him, 'Assuredly, I say to you today,* you will be with Me in Paradise.'" Luke 23:42, 43.

---

* By placing the comma after the word "today" instead of after the word "you," as in the common versions, the true meaning of the text is more apparent. Jesus Himself said on the following Sunday morning that He had not yet ascended to His Father. John 20:17.

With amazement the angels saw the infinite love of Jesus who, while suffering the most excruciating agony of mind and body, thought only of others and encouraged the penitent sinner to believe. While pouring out His life in death, He exercised a love for lost human beings that is stronger than death. Many who witnessed those scenes on Calvary found later that these events established them in the faith of Christ.

The enemies of Jesus now waited for His death with impatient hope. They imagined that His death would forever hush the rumors of His divine power and the wonders of His miracles. They told themselves that then they would no longer tremble because of His influence. The unfeeling soldiers who had stretched the body of Jesus on the cross divided His clothing among themselves, arguing over one garment, which was woven without seam. They finally decided the matter by gambling for it. Inspiration had accurately described this scene hundreds of years before it took place: "For dogs have surrounded Me; the congregation of the wicked has enclosed Me. They pierced My hands and My feet; . . . they divide My garments among them, and for My clothing they cast lots." Psalm 22:16, 18.

A Lesson in Love for Parents—The eyes of Jesus wandered over the crowd that had gathered to witness His death, and at the foot of the cross He saw John supporting Mary, the mother of Christ. She had returned to the terrible scene, not being able to remain away from her Son any longer. The last lesson of Jesus was about love for one's parents. He looked at the grief-stricken face of His mother, and then at John. Looking again at His mother, He said, "Woman, behold your son!" Then, to the disciple, "Behold your mother!" John 19:26, 27. John well understood Jesus' words and the sacred trust He was committing to him. He immediately took the mother of Christ away from the fearful scene of Calvary. From that hour he cared for her as a dutiful son would, taking her to his own home. The perfect example of Christ's filial love shines undimmed from the mist of ages. While enduring the keenest torture, He was not forgetful of His mother, but made all necessary provision for her future.

The mission of Christ's earthly life was now nearly accomplished. His tongue was parched, and He said, "I thirst!" They saturated a sponge with vinegar and gall and offered it to Him to drink; and when He had tasted it, He refused it. And now the Lord of life and glory was dying, a ransom for the race. It was the sense of sin, bringing the Father's wrath upon Him as our substitute, that made the cup He drank so bitter, and broke the heart of the Son of God.

The iniquity of the human race was laid upon Christ as our substitute. He was counted as a transgressor so that He could redeem transgressors from the curse of the law. The guilt of every descendant of Adam from every age was pressing on His heart. The wrath of God and the terrible manifestation of His displeasure because of iniquity filled the soul of His Son with dismay. The withdrawal of the Father's face from the Savior in this hour of supreme anguish pierced His heart with a sorrow that human beings can never fully understand. Every pang that the Son of God endured on the cross, the blood drops that flowed from His head, His hands and feet, the convulsions of agony that racked His frame, and the unutterable anguish that filled His soul at the hiding of His Father's face from Him, speak to us, saying, It is for love of you that the Son of God consents to have these terrible crimes laid on Him. For you He plunders the domain of death and opens the gates of Paradise and immortal life. He who stilled the angry waves by His word and walked the foam-capped billows, who made devils tremble and disease flee from His touch, who raised the dead to life and opened the eyes of the blind, offers Himself on the cross as the last sacrifice for sinners. He, the sin-bearer, endures judicial punishment for iniquity and becomes sin itself for our sake.

Satan wrung the heart of Jesus with his fierce temptations. Sin, so hateful to His sight, was heaped on Him till He groaned beneath its weight. No wonder that His humanity trembled in that fearful hour. Angels witnessed with amazement the despairing agony of the Son of God, so much greater than His physical pain that He hardly felt the latter. The hosts of heaven veiled their faces from the fearful sight.

Inanimate nature expressed a sympathy with its insulted and dying Author. The sun refused to look upon the awful scene. Its full, bright rays were illuminating the earth at midday, when suddenly it seemed to be blotted out. Complete darkness enveloped the cross and all the surrounding vicinity, like a funeral pall. The darkness lasted three full hours. At the ninth hour the terrible darkness lifted from the people, but still wrapped the Savior as if in a mantle. The angry lightnings seemed to be hurled at Him as He hung on the cross. Then "Jesus cried out with a loud voice, saying, 'Eloi, Eloi, lama sabachthani?' which is translated, 'My God, My God, why have You forsaken Me?' " Mark 15:34.

It Is Finished—In silence the people watch for the end of this fearful scene. Again the sun shines, but the cross is enveloped in darkness. Suddenly the gloom lifts from the cross, and in clear trumpet tones that seem to echo throughout creation, Jesus cries, "It is finished!" "Father, 'into Your hands I commit My spirit.' " Luke 23:46. A light encircled the cross, and the face of the Savior shone with a glory like the sun. He then bowed His head upon His breast and died.

At the moment in which Christ died, there were priests ministering in the temple before the veil that separated the holy place from the most holy place. Suddenly they felt the earth tremble beneath them, and the veil of the temple, a strong rich drapery, was torn in two from top to bottom by the same bloodless hand that wrote the words of doom on the walls of Belshazzar's palace.

Jesus did not yield up His life until He had accomplished the work that He came to do, and then He exclaimed with His parting breath, "It is finished!" Angels rejoiced to hear those words, for the great plan of redemption was being triumphantly carried out. There was joy in heaven that now, through a life of obedience, the children of Adam could be exalted finally to the presence of God. Satan was defeated. He knew that his kingdom was lost.

The Burial—John was puzzled to know what to do about the body of his beloved Master. He shuddered at the thought of its being handled by rough and unfeeling soldiers and placed in a dishonored burial place. He knew he could obtain no favors from the Jewish authorities, and he had little hope of anything from Pilate. But Joseph and Nicodemus came forward in this emergency. Both of them were members of the Sanhedrin and were acquainted with Pilate. Both had wealth and influence. They were determined that the body of Jesus should have an honorable burial.

Joseph went boldly to Pilate and asked him for the body of Jesus for burial. Pilate then gave an official order for the body of Jesus to be given to Joseph. While the disciple John was anxious and troubled about the sacred remains of his beloved Master, Joseph of Arimathea returned with the commission from the governor, and Nicodemus, anticipating the result of Joseph's interview with Pilate, came with a costly mixture of myrrh and aloes, about one hundred pounds' weight. The most honored in all Jerusalem could not have been shown more respect in death.

Gently and reverently, with their own hands they removed the body of Jesus from the instrument of torture, their sympathetic tears falling fast as they looked on His bruised and lacerated form, which they carefully bathed and cleansed from the stain of blood. Joseph owned a new tomb, hewn from stone, which he was reserving for himself. It was near Calvary, and he now prepared this sepulcher for Jesus. The body, together with the spices Nicodemus had brought, was carefully wrapped in a linen sheet, and the three disciples bore their precious burden to the new sepulcher, in which no one had ever been buried before. There they straightened those mangled limbs and folded the bruised hands on the pulseless breast. The Galilean women came near, to see that everything had been done that could be done for the lifeless form of their beloved Teacher. Then they saw the heavy stone rolled against the entrance of the sepulcher, and the Son of God was left at rest. The women were last at the cross, and last at the tomb of Christ.

Although the Jewish rulers had carried out their devilish plan in putting to death the Son of God, their uneasiness did not go away, nor was their jealousy of Christ dead. Mingled with the joy of gratified revenge, they felt an ever-present fear that His dead body, lying in Joseph's tomb, would come out to life. Therefore "the chief priests and Pharisees gathered together to Pilate, saying, 'Sir, we remember, while He was still alive, how that deceiver said, "After three days I will rise." Therefore command that the tomb be made secure until the third day, lest His disciples come by night and steal Him away, and say to the people, "He has risen from the dead." So the last deception will be worse than the first.' " Matthew 27:62-64. Pilate was as unwilling as the Jews were to have Jesus rise with power to punish the guilt of those who had destroyed Him, so he placed a band of Roman soldiers at the command of the priests.

The Jews realized the advantage of having such a guard around the tomb of Jesus. They placed a seal on the stone that closed the sepulcher so that it could not be disturbed without the fact being known, taking every precaution against the disciples' practicing any deception regarding the body of Jesus. But all their plans and precautions only served to make the triumph of the resurrection more complete and to establish its truth more fully.

Chapter 9

The Conquest

RESURRECTION

The disciples rested on the Sabbath, mourning the death of their Lord, while Jesus, the King of glory, lay in the tomb. As night approached, soldiers were stationed to guard the Savior's resting place, while angels hovered unseen above the sacred spot. The night wore slowly away, and while it was yet dark the watching angels knew that the time had nearly come for the release of God's Son, their loved Commander. As they were waiting with the deepest emotion for the hour of His triumph, a mighty angel came flying swiftly from heaven. His face was like the lightning, and his garments white as snow. His light dispelled the darkness from his track and caused the evil angels, who had triumphantly claimed the body of Jesus, to flee in terror from his brightness and glory. One of the angels who had witnessed the scene of Christ's humiliation and was watching His resting place joined the angel from heaven, and together they came down to the sepulcher. The earth trembled and shook as they approached, and there was a great earthquake.

Terror seized the Roman guard. Where now was their power to keep the body of Jesus? They did not think of their duty or of the disciples' stealing Him away. As the light of the angels shone around them, brighter than the sun, that Roman guard fell to the ground like dead men. One of the angels laid hold of the great stone, rolled it away from the door of the sepulcher, and seated himself on it. The other entered the tomb and untied the cloth from the head of Jesus.

"Your Father Calls You"—Then, with a voice that caused the earth to quake, the angel from heaven cried out, "O Son of God, Your Father calls You! Come out!" Death could hold dominion over Him no longer. Jesus arose from the dead, a triumphant conqueror. In solemn awe the gathered angels gazed on the scene. And as Jesus came out from the sepulcher, those shining angels bowed themselves to the earth in worship and greeted Him with songs of victory and triumph.

The Report of the Roman Guard—As the host of heavenly angels left the tomb and the light and glory passed away, the Roman guard ventured to raise their heads and look about them. They were filled with amazement as they saw that the great stone had been rolled from the door of the sepulcher and that the body of Jesus was gone. They hurried to the city to make known to the priests and elders what they had seen. As those murderers listened to the marvelous report, paleness marked every face. Horror seized them at the thought of what they had done. If the report was correct, they were lost. For a time they sat in silence, looking at one another's faces, not knowing what to do or what to say. To accept the report would be to condemn themselves. They went aside to consult regarding what to do. They reasoned that if the report of the guard were to circulate among the people, those who put Christ to death would be killed as His murderers.

They decided to hire the soldiers to keep the matter secret. The priests and elders offered them a large sum of money, saying, "Tell them, 'His disciples came at night and stole Him away while we slept.'" Matthew 28:13. And when the guard asked what would happen to them for sleeping at their post, the Jewish officers promised to persuade the governor and secure their safety. For the sake of money, the Roman guard sold their honor and agreed to follow the counsel of the priests and elders.

The First Fruits of Redemption—When Jesus, hanging on the cross, cried out, "It is finished," the rocks split, the earth shook, and some of the graves were opened. When He arose a victor over death and the grave, while the earth was reeling and the glory of heaven shone around the sacred spot, many of the righteous dead, obedient to His call, came out from their graves as witnesses that He had risen. Those favored, risen saints came out glorified. They were chosen and holy ones of every age, from creation down even to the days of Christ. So while the Jewish leaders were seeking to conceal the fact of Christ's resurrection, God chose to bring up a company from their graves to testify that Jesus had risen, and to declare His glory.

Those who came to life after the resurrection of Jesus appeared to many, telling them that the sacrifice for mankind was completed, that Jesus, whom the Jews crucified, had risen from the dead. In proof of their words they declared, "We are risen with Him." They testified that it was by His mighty power that they had been called from their graves. Despite the lying reports that circulated, the resurrection of Christ could not be concealed by Satan, his angels, or the chief priests, for this holy company, brought out from their graves, spread the wonderful, joyful news. Jesus also showed Himself to His sorrowing, heartbroken disciples, dispelling their fears and causing them joy and gladness.

The Women at the Sepulcher—Early in the morning of the first day of the week, before it was yet light, devout women came to the sepulcher, bringing sweet spices to anoint the body of Jesus. They found that the heavy stone had been rolled away from the door of the sepulcher, and the body of Jesus was not there. Their hearts sank within them, and they feared that their enemies had taken away the body. Suddenly they saw two angels in white clothing, their faces bright and shining. These heavenly beings understood what the women had come to do, and immediately they told them that Jesus was not there. He had risen, but they could see the place where He had lain. They told them to go and tell His disciples that He would go ahead of them into Galilee. With fear and great joy, the women hurried back to the sorrowing disciples and told them the things they had seen and heard.

The disciples could not believe that Christ had risen, but

they ran quickly to the sepulcher, along with the women who had brought the report. They found that Jesus was not there. They saw His linen grave-clothes but could not believe the good news that He had risen from the dead. They returned home, marveling at what they had seen, and also at the report the women had brought them.

But Mary chose to linger around the sepulcher, thinking of what she had seen and feeling distressed with the thought that she might have been deceived. She felt that new trials awaited her. Her grief revived, and she broke out in bitter weeping. She stooped down to look again into the sepulcher, and there she saw two angels clothed in white. One was sitting where the head of Jesus had lain, the other where His feet had been. They spoke to her tenderly and asked her why she wept. She replied, "Because they have taken away my Lord, and I do not know where they have laid Him." John 20:13.

"Do Not Cling to Me"—As she turned from the sepulcher she saw Jesus standing near, but she did not recognize Him. He spoke to her tenderly, inquiring why she was sorrowful and asking whom she was seeking. Supposing that He was the gardener, she asked Him, if He had carried away her Lord, to tell her where He had laid Him, so that she could take Him away. Jesus spoke to her with his own heavenly voice, saying, "Mary!" She knew the tones of that dear voice and quickly answered, "Master!" In her joy she was about to embrace Him, but Jesus said, "Do not cling to Me, for I have not yet ascended to My Father; but go to My brethren and say to them, 'I am ascending to My Father and your Father, and to My God and your God.' " John 20:17. Joyfully she hurried to the disciples with the good news. Jesus quickly ascended to His Father to hear from His lips that He accepted the sacrifice and to receive all power in heaven and on earth.

While Jesus was in the presence of God and surrounded by His glory, He did not forget His disciples on the earth. He received power from His Father so that He could return and give power to them. The same day He returned and showed

Himself to His disciples. He allowed them then to touch Him, for He had ascended to His Father and had received power.

Doubting Thomas—At this time Thomas was not present. He would not humbly receive the report of the disciples, but firmly and self-confidently affirmed that he would not believe unless he could put his fingers in the prints of the nails and his hand in the side where the cruel spear was thrust. In this he showed a lack of confidence in his brethren. If everyone were to require the same evidence, no one today would receive Jesus and believe in His resurrection. But it was the will of God that those who could not themselves see and hear the risen Savior should receive the report of the disciples.

God was not pleased with Thomas's unbelief. When Jesus met with His disciples again, Thomas was with them, and when he saw Jesus, he believed. But he had declared that he would not be satisfied without having the evidence of feeling added to sight, and Jesus gave him the evidence he had wanted. Thomas cried out, "My Lord and my God!" But Jesus reproved him for his unbelief, saying, "Thomas, because you have seen Me, you have believed. Blessed are those who have not seen and yet have believed." John 20:28, 29.

The Downfall of Christ's Slayer—As the news spread from city to city and from town to town, the Jewish leaders feared for their lives and concealed their hatred for the disciples. Their only hope was to spread their lying report. And those who wished this lie to be true accepted it. Pilate trembled as he heard that Christ had risen. He could not doubt the testimony given, and from that hour peace left him forever. For the sake of worldly honor, for fear of losing his authority and his life, he had condemned Jesus to die. He was now fully convinced that he was guilty not merely of the blood of an innocent man, but of the Son of God. Miserable to its close was the life of Pilate. Despair and anguish crushed every hopeful, joyful feeling. He refused to be comforted, and he died a most miserable death.

Forty Days With the Disciples—Jesus remained with His disciples forty days, causing them joy and gladness as He opened to them more fully the realities of the kingdom of God. He commissioned them to bear testimony to the things they had seen and heard concerning His sufferings, death, and resurrection. They were to tell that He had made a sacrifice for sin, and that all who wanted to could come to Him and find life. With faithful tenderness He told them that they would be persecuted and distressed, but they would find relief in recalling their experience and remembering the words He had spoken to them. He told them that He had overcome the temptations of Satan and had obtained the victory through trials and suffering. Satan could have no more power over Him, but he would bring his temptations to bear more directly on them and on all who would believe in His name. But they could overcome as He had overcome. Jesus endowed His disciples with power to work miracles, and He told them that although they would be persecuted by wicked men, from time to time He would send His angels to deliver them; their lives could not be taken until their mission was accomplished. Then they might be required to seal with their blood the testimonies they had borne.

His anxious followers gladly listened to His teachings, eagerly feasting on every word that came from His holy lips. Now they knew for certain that He was the Savior of the world. His words sank deep into their hearts, and they were sad that they must soon be separated from their heavenly Teacher and no longer hear His comforting, gracious words. But again their hearts were warmed with love and great joy, as Jesus told them that He would go and prepare places for them and come again and receive them, that they could always be with Him. He also promised to send the Comforter, the Holy Spirit, to guide them into all truth. "And He lifted up His hands and blessed them." Luke 24:50.

THE ASCENSION OF CHRIST

All heaven was awaiting the hour of triumph when Jesus

would ascend to His Father. Angels came to receive the King of glory and to escort Him triumphantly to heaven. After Jesus had blessed His disciples, He was parted from them and taken up. And as He led the way upward, the multitude of captives who were raised at His resurrection followed. A large gathering of the heavenly angels accompanied them, while in heaven an innumerable company of angels awaited His coming.

Then all the heavenly host surrounded their majestic Commander and bowed before Him with the deepest adoration, casting their glittering crowns at His feet. And then they touched their golden harps, and in sweet, melodious tones filled all heaven with rich music and songs to the Lamb who was slain, yet who lives again in majesty and glory.

The Promise of Return—As the disciples gazed sorrowfully toward heaven to catch the last glimpse of their ascending Lord, two angels clothed in white apparel stood by them and said to them, "Men of Galilee, why do you stand gazing up into heaven? This same Jesus, who was taken up from you into heaven, will so come in like manner as you saw Him go into heaven." Acts 1:11. The disciples talked over His wonderful acts and the strange and glorious events that had taken place within a short time.

The Anger of Satan—Satan again counseled with his angels, and with bitter hatred against God's government told them that while he retained his power and authority on earth, their efforts must be ten times stronger against the followers of Jesus. They had won in no attack against Christ but must overthrow His followers, if possible. In every generation they must seek to trap those who would believe in Jesus. Then Satan's angels went out like roaring lions, seeking to destroy the followers of Jesus.

Chapter 10

The Power

When Jesus opened the understanding of the disciples to the meaning of the prophecies about Himself, He assured them that all power was given Him in heaven and on earth, and He told them to go and preach the gospel to every creature. With a sudden revival of their old hope that Jesus would take His place on the throne of David at Jerusalem, the disciples asked Him, "Lord, will You at this time restore the kingdom to Israel?" Acts 1:6. The Savior left them uncertain about this by replying that it was not for them "to know times or seasons which the Father has put in His own authority." Acts 1:7.

The disciples began to hope that the wonderful descent of the Holy Spirit would influence the Jewish people to accept Jesus. The Savior declined to explain further, for He knew that when the Holy Spirit would come on them in full measure, their minds would be illuminated. They would fully understand the work before them and take it up just where He had left it.

The disciples assembled in the upper room, uniting in prayer with the believing women, with Mary the mother of Jesus, and with His brothers. These brothers, who had been unbelieving, were now fully established in their faith by the scenes attending the crucifixion and by the resurrection and ascension of the Lord. The number assembled was about one hundred twenty.

The Descent of the Holy Spirit—"When the Day of Pentecost had fully come, they were all with one accord in one place. And suddenly there came a sound from heaven, as of a rushing mighty wind, and it filled the whole house where they

This chapter is based on Acts 2.

• 83 •

were sitting. Then there appeared to them divided tongues, as of fire, and one sat upon each of them. And they were all filled with the Holy Spirit and began to speak with other tongues, as the Spirit gave them utterance." The Holy Spirit, taking the form of tongues of fire divided at the tips and resting on the assembled group, was a sign of the gift bestowed on them of speaking fluently several different languages that they had not known before. And the appearance of fire signified the fervent zeal with which they would labor and the power that would accompany their words.

Under this heavenly illumination, the scriptures that Christ had explained to them stood out in their minds with the vivid luster and loveliness of clear and powerful truth. The veil that had prevented them from seeing what Christ had abolished was now removed, and they understood the object of Christ's mission and the nature of His kingdom with perfect clearness.

In the Power of Pentecost—The Jews had been scattered to almost every nation, and they spoke various languages. They had come long distances to Jerusalem and were staying there temporarily for the religious festivals then in progress and to fulfill their requirements. The worshipers assembled there were of every known tongue. This diversity of languages was a great obstacle to the labors of God's servants in spreading the doctrine of Christ to the farthest parts of the earth. But God filled the need of the apostles in a miraculous way, and to the people this most perfectly confirmed the testimony of these witnesses for Christ. The Holy Spirit had done for them what they could not have accomplished for themselves in a lifetime. Now they could spread the truth of the gospel far and wide, speaking with accuracy the language of those for whom they were ministering. This miraculous gift was the highest evidence they could present to the world that their commission bore the approval of Heaven.

"And there were dwelling in Jerusalem Jews, devout men, from every nation under heaven. And when this sound occurred, the multitude came together, and were confused, because everyone heard them speak in his own language. Then they were all amazed and marveled, saying to one another, 'Look, are not all these who speak Galileans? And how is it that we hear, each in our own language in which we were born?"

The priests and rulers were greatly enraged at this amazing development, which was reported throughout all Jerusalem and the vicinity. Yet they did not dare to act on their evil intentions for fear of exposing themselves to the hatred of the people. They had put the Master to death, but here were His servants, uneducated men from Galilee, outlining the astonishing fulfillment of prophecy and teaching the doctrine of Jesus in all the languages then spoken. They spoke with power of the Savior's wonderful works and opened to their hearers the plan of salvation in the mercy and sacrifice of the Son of God. Their words convicted and converted thousands who listened. The traditions and superstitions that the priests taught were swept away from their minds, and they accepted the pure teachings of the Word of God.

Peter's Sermon—Peter showed them that what they were seeing was the direct fulfillment of the prophecy of Joel, in which he foretold that such power would come upon people of God to fit them for a special work.

Peter traced the ancestry of Christ in a direct line back to the honorable house of David. He did not use any of the teachings of Jesus to prove His true position, because he knew their prejudices were so great that it would be of no effect. But he referred them to David, whom the Jews regarded as a highly respected patriarch of their nation. Peter said:

"For David says concerning Him: 'I foresaw the Lord always before my face, for He is at my right hand, that I may not be shaken. Therefore my heart rejoiced, and my tongue was glad; moreover my flesh also will rest in hope. For You will not leave my soul in Hades, nor will You allow Your Holy One to see corruption.' "

Here Peter shows that David could not have spoken about

himself, but definitely of Jesus Christ. David died a natural death like other people. His tomb, with the honored dust it contained, had been preserved with great care until that time. As king of Israel and also as a prophet, David had been specially honored by God. In prophetic vision God showed him the future life and ministry of Christ. He saw His rejection, His trial, crucifixion, burial, resurrection, and ascension.

David testified that the soul of Christ was not to be left in Hades (the grave), nor was His flesh to see corruption. Peter showed that Jesus of Nazareth fulfilled this prophecy. God had actually raised Him up from the tomb before His body saw decay. He was now the exalted One in the highest heavens.

On that memorable occasion, large numbers who until then had ridiculed the idea of so humble a person as Jesus being the Son of God became thoroughly convinced of the truth and acknowledged Him as their Savior. Three thousand people were added to the church. The apostles spoke by the power of the Holy Spirit, and no one could argue with their words. Their messages were confirmed by mighty miracles, which they did through the outpouring of the Spirit of God. The disciples themselves were astonished at the results of this display of God's power and the quick and large harvest of believers. All the people were filled with amazement. Those who did not yield their prejudice and bigotry were so over-awed that they did not dare to try to stop the mighty work, whether by voice or violence, and their opposition ended for the time being.

The arguments of the apostles alone, clear and convincing as they were, would not have removed the prejudice of the Jews that had withstood so much evidence. But the Holy Spirit sent those arguments home to their hearts with divine power. They were like sharp arrows of the Almighty, convicting them of their terrible guilt in rejecting and crucifying the Lord of glory. "Now when they heard this, they were cut to the heart, and said to Peter and the rest of the apostles, 'Men and brethren, what shall we do?' Then Peter said to them, 'Repent, and let every one of you be baptized in the name of

Jesus Christ for the remission of sins; and you shall receive the gift of the Holy Spirit.' "

Peter urged upon the convicted people the fact that they had rejected Christ because they had been deceived by the priests and rulers. If they continued to look to them for counsel and waited for those leaders to acknowledge Christ before they dared to do so, they would never accept Him. Although those powerful men made a profession of sanctity, they were ambitious and zealous for riches and earthly glory. They would never come to Christ to receive light. Jesus had foretold a terrible punishment to come upon that people for their obstinate unbelief, in spite of the most powerful evidences given them that Jesus was the Son of God.

From this time onward, the language of the disciples was pure, simple, and accurate in word and accent, whether they spoke their native tongue or a foreign language. These humble men, who had never studied in the school of the prophets, presented truths so elevated and pure as to astonish those who heard them. They could not go personally to the ends of the earth, but there were people at the feast from every quarter of the world, and they carried the truths they received to their various homes and spread them among their people, winning converts to Christ.

A Lesson for Our Day—We have this testimony about the establishment of the Christian church not only as an important portion of sacred history but also as a lesson. All who profess the name of Christ should be waiting, watching, and praying with one heart. We should put away all differences and let unity and tender love one for another pervade everything. Then our prayers can go up together to our heavenly Father with strong, earnest faith. Then we may wait for the fulfillment of the promise with patience and hope.

The answer may come with sudden speed and overpowering might, or it may be delayed for days and weeks, and our faith be tested. But God knows how and when to answer our prayer. It is our part of the work to put ourselves in connection with the divine channel. God is responsible for His part of the work. He who has promised is faithful. The great and important matter with us is to be of one heart and mind, putting aside all envy and malice, and, as humble people of prayer, to watch and wait. Jesus, our Representative and Head, is ready to do for us what He did for the praying, watching ones on the day of Pentecost.

Chapter 11

The Apostasy

When Jesus revealed to His disciples the fate of Jerusalem and the scenes of His second advent, He also foretold the experience of His people from the time when He would be taken from them to His return in power and glory for their deliverance. From the Mount of Olives, the Savior saw the storms about to fall on the church the apostles would establish, and, looking deeper into the future, His eye saw the fierce, destructive tempests that were to beat upon His followers in the coming ages of darkness and persecution. In a few brief statements, dreadfully significant, He foretold the troubles that the rulers of this world would inflict on the church of God. The followers of Christ must walk the same path of humiliation, condemnation, and suffering that their Master walked. The hatred that burst forth against the world's Redeemer would be displayed against all who would believe on His name.

The history of the early church testified to the accuracy of the Savior's words. The powers of earth and hell arrayed themselves against Christ in the person of His followers. Paganism foresaw that if the gospel were to triumph, her temples and altars would be swept away. Therefore she marshalled her forces to destroy Christianity. The fires of persecution were kindled. Christians were stripped of their possessions and driven from their homes. They "endured a great struggle with sufferings." They "had trial of mockings and scourgings, yes, and of chains and imprisonment." Hebrews 10:32, 11:36. Great numbers sealed their testimony with their blood. Noble and slave, rich and poor, educated and ignorant, were alike killed without mercy.

Satan's efforts to destroy the church of Christ by violence

were in vain. The great controversy in which the disciples of Jesus yielded up their lives did not end when these faithful standard-bearers fell at their post. By defeat they conquered. God's workmen were killed, but His work went steadily forward. The gospel continued to spread, and the number of its adherents continued to increase. It penetrated into regions that were inaccessible, even to the armies of Rome. Said a Christian, appealing to the heathen rulers who were pressing forward with the persecution: You may "kill us, torture us, condemn us. . . . Your injustice is the proof that we are innocent. . . . Nor does your cruelty . . . help you." It became a stronger invitation to bring others to belief in Christ. "The more often we are mown down by you, the more in number we grow; the blood of Christians is seed."

Thousands were imprisoned and killed, but others sprang up to fill their places. And those who were martyred for their faith were secured to Christ, and He accounted them as conquerors. They had fought the good fight, and they were to receive the crown of glory when Christ would come. The sufferings they endured brought Christians nearer to one another and to their Redeemer. Their living example and dying testimony were a constant witness for the truth; and, where least expected, the subjects of Satan were leaving his service and enlisting under the banner of Christ.

The Compromise With Paganism—Satan therefore laid his plans to battle more successfully against the government of God, by planting his banner in the Christian church. If the followers of Christ could be deceived and led to displease God, then their strength, endurance, and firmness would fail, and they would be easy prey for Satan.

The great adversary now tried to gain by deception what he had failed to secure by force. Persecution ended, and in its place he substituted the dangerous allurements of temporal prosperity and worldly honor. Idol-worshipers were led to receive a part of the Christian faith, while they rejected other essential truths. They professed to accept Jesus as the Son of

God and to believe in His death and resurrection, but they had no conviction of sin and felt no need of repentance or of a change of heart. With some concessions on their part, they proposed that Christians also should make concessions, so that all might unite on the platform of belief in Christ.

Now the church was in fearful danger. Prison, torture, fire, and sword were blessings in comparison with this. Some of the Christians stood firm, declaring that they could make no compromise. Others reasoned that if they yielded or modified some features of their faith and united with those who had accepted a part of Christianity, it might be the means of their full conversion. That was a time of deep anguish to the faithful followers of Christ. Under a cover of pretended Christianity, Satan was subtly maneuvering himself into the church, to corrupt their faith and turn their minds from the word of truth.

At last the larger portion of Christians lowered their standard and formed a union between Christianity and paganism. Although the worshipers of idols professed to be converted, and they united with the church, they still clung to their idolatry, only changing the objects of their worship to images of Jesus, and even of Mary and the saints. The foul leaven of idolatry, introduced this way into the church, continued its destructive work. Unsound doctrines, superstitious rites, and idolatrous ceremonies were incorporated into the church's faith and worship. As the followers of Christ united with idolaters, the Christian religion became corrupted and the church lost her purity and power. There were some, however, who were not misled by these delusions. They still maintained their faithfulness to the Author of truth and worshiped God alone.

There have always been two classes among those who profess to be followers of Christ. While the people in one class study the Savior's life and earnestly seek to correct their defects and to conform to the Pattern, those in the other class shun the plain, practical truths that expose their errors. Even in her best times the church was not composed entirely of the true, pure, and sincere. Our Savior taught that those who willfully indulge in sin are not to be received into the church. Yet He connected with Himself men with faulty characters, and He granted them the benefits of His teachings and example, to give them an opportunity to see and correct their errors.

But there is no union between the Prince of light and the prince of darkness, and there can be no union between their followers. When Christians consented to unite with those who were only half converted from paganism, they started down a path that led farther and farther from the truth. Satan rejoiced that he had succeeded in deceiving so many of the followers of Christ. He then brought his power to bear on them even more, inspiring them to persecute those who remained true to God. None could understand so well how to oppose the true Christian faith as could those who had once been its defenders. These apostate Christians, uniting with their half-pagan companions, directed their warfare against the most essential features of the doctrines of Christ.

Those who wanted to be faithful found that it required a desperate struggle to stand firm against the deceptions and abominations that were disguised in priestly garments and introduced into the church. The Bible was no longer accepted as the standard of faith. The doctrine of religious freedom was termed heresy, and its upholders were hated and condemned.

Necessary Separation—After a long and severe conflict the faithful few decided to sever all connection with the apostate church if she still refused to free herself from falsehood and idolatry. They saw that separation was absolutely necessary if they were going to obey the Word of God. They dared not tolerate errors fatal to their own souls and set an example that would imperil the faith of their children and children's children. To secure peace and unity, they were ready to make any concession consistent with being true to God, but they felt that even peace would be too expensive if it meant sacrificing principle. If unity could come only by the compromise of truth and righteousness, then let there be difference, and even war. Well would it be for the church and the world if the principles that actuated those steadfast believers were revived in the hearts of God's professed people.

The apostle Paul declares that "all who desire to live godly in Christ Jesus will suffer persecution." 2 Timothy 3:12. Why is it, then, that to a great degree persecution seems to be asleep? The only reason is that the church has conformed to the world's standard, and therefore it awakens no opposition. The religion current in our day is not of the pure and holy character that marked the Christian faith in the days of Christ and His apostles. It is only because of the spirit of compromise with sin, because the great truths of the Word of God are regarded with such indifference, because there is so little vital godliness in the church, that Christianity is apparently so popular with the world. Let there be a revival of the faith and power of the early church, and the spirit of persecution will revive and the fires of persecution will be rekindled.

THE MYSTERY OF INIQUITY

In his second letter to the Thessalonians, the apostle Paul foretold the great apostasy that would result in the establishment of the papal power. He declared that the day of Christ would not come "unless the falling away comes first, and the man of sin is revealed, the son of perdition, who opposes and exalts himself above all that is called God or that is worshiped, so that he sits as God in the temple of God, showing himself that he is God." And furthermore, the apostle warns his fellow believers that "the mystery of lawlessness is already at work." 2 Thessalonians 2:3, 4, 7. Even at that early date he saw, creeping into the church, errors that would prepare the way for the development of the Papacy.

Little by little, at first in stealth and silence and then more openly as it increased in strength and gained control of human minds, the mystery of iniquity carried forward its deceptive and blasphemous work. Almost imperceptibly the customs of heathenism found their way into the Christian church. The spirit of compromise and conformity was held back for a time by the fierce persecutions that the church endured under paganism. But as persecution ended, and Christianity entered the courts and palaces of kings, she laid aside the humble simplicity of Christ and His apostles for the pomp and pride of pagan priests and rulers, and in place of the requirements of God she substituted human theories and traditions. The nominal conversion of Constantine in the early part of the fourth century caused great rejoicing, and the world, arrayed in robes of righteousness, walked into the church. Now the work of corruption rapidly progressed. Paganism, while appearing to be vanquished, became the conqueror. Her spirit controlled the church. Her doctrines, ceremonies, and superstitions were incorporated into the faith and worship of the professed followers of Christ.

This compromise between paganism and Christianity resulted in the development of the man of sin foretold in prophecy as opposing and exalting himself above God. That gigantic system of false religion is a masterpiece of Satan's power—a monument of his efforts to seat himself on the throne to rule the earth according to his will.

It is one of the leading doctrines of Romanism that the pope is the visible head of the universal church of Christ, invested with supreme authority over bishops and pastors in all parts of the world. More than this, the pope has taken to himself the very titles of Deity.

Satan well knew that the Holy Scriptures would enable people to discern his deceptions and withstand his power. It was by the Word that even the Savior of the world had resisted his attacks. At every assault Christ presented the shield of eternal truth, saying, "It is written." To every suggestion of the adversary he countered with the wisdom and power of the Word. In order for Satan to maintain his influence over people and establish the authority of the papal usurper, he must keep them in ignorance of the Scriptures. The Bible would exalt God and place finite men and women in their true position. For this reason, its sacred truths must be concealed and suppressed. This logic was adopted by the Roman church. For hundreds of years it prohibited the circulation of the Bible. The people were forbidden to read it or to have it in their houses, and unprincipled priests and prelates interpreted its teachings to sustain their claims. In this way the pope came to be almost universally acknowledged as the vicegerent of God on earth, endowed with supreme authority over church and state.

Times and Laws Changed—The detector of error having been removed, Satan worked according to his will. Prophecy had declared that the Papacy was to "intend to change times and law." Daniel 7:25. This work it was not slow to attempt. To offer converts from heathenism a substitute for the worship of idols, and so to promote their nominal acceptance of Christianity, the adoration of images and relics was gradually introduced into the Christian worship. The decree of a general council finally established this system of idolatry. To complete the sacrilegious work, Rome presumed to expunge from the law of God the second commandment, which forbids image worship, and to divide the tenth commandment, in order to preserve the number.

The spirit of concession to paganism opened the way for a still further disregard of Heaven's authority. Satan tampered with the fourth commandment also, and purposed to set aside the ancient Sabbath, the day that God had blessed and sanctified, and in its place to exalt the festival observed by the heathen as "the venerable day of the sun." This change was not at first attempted openly. In the first centuries all Christians had kept the true Sabbath. They were jealous for the honor of God, and, believing that His law is unchangeable, they zealously guarded the sacredness of its precepts. But Satan worked very subtly through his agents to bring about his objective. To call the attention of the people to the Sunday, it was made a festival in honor of the resurrection of Christ. Religious services were held on it, yet it was regarded as a day of recreation, and the Sabbath was still being sacredly observed.

While he was still a heathen, Constantine issued a decree requiring the general observance of Sunday as a public festival throughout the Roman Empire. After his conversion he remained a staunch advocate of Sunday, and he then enforced his pagan edict in the interests of his new faith. But the honor shown this day was not as yet sufficient to prevent Christians from regarding the true Sabbath as the holy of the Lord. Another step must be taken: the false sabbath must be exalted to be equal with the true. A few years after Constantine issued his decree, the Bishop of Rome conferred on the Sunday the title of Lord's day. In this way the people were gradually led to regard it as having a degree of sacredness. Still the original Sabbath was kept.

The arch-deceiver had not completed his work. He was determined to gather the Christian world under his banner and to exercise his power through his vicegerent, the proud pontiff who claimed to be the representative of Christ. Through half-converted pagans, ambitious prelates, and world-loving churchmen he accomplished his purpose. From time to time vast councils were held, in which the dignitaries of the church convened from all the world. In nearly every council the Sabbath that God had instituted was pressed down a little lower, while the Sunday was correspondingly exalted. This is how the pagan festival came finally to be honored as a divine institution, while the Bible Sabbath was pronounced a relic of Judaism, and its observers were declared to be accursed.

The great apostate had succeeded in exalting himself "above all that is called God or that is worshiped." 2 Thessalonians 2:4. He had dared to change the only precept of the divine law that unmistakably points all mankind to the true and living God. In the fourth commandment God is revealed as the Creator of the heavens and the earth, which distinguishes Him from all false gods. It was as a memorial of the work of creation that the seventh day was sanctified as a rest day for man. It was designed to keep the living God always before human minds as the source of everything and the object of reverence and worship. Satan tries to turn people from their allegiance to God and from obedience to His law. Therefore he directs his efforts especially against the one commandment that points to God as the Creator.

Protestants now urge that the resurrection of Christ on Sunday made it the Christian Sabbath. But Scripture evidence is lacking. No such honor was given to the day by Christ or His apostles. The observance of Sunday as a Christian institution has its origin in that "mystery of lawlessness" which had begun its work even in Paul's day. Where and when did the Lord adopt this child of the Papacy? What valid reason can be given for a change on which the Scriptures are silent?

In the sixth century the Papacy had become firmly established. Its seat of power was fixed in the imperial city, and the Bishop of Rome was declared to be the head over the entire church. Paganism had given place to the Papacy. The dragon had given to the beast "his power, his throne, and great authority." Revelation 13:2. And now began the 1260 years of papal oppression foretold in the prophecies of Daniel and John. (Daniel 7:25; Revelation 13:5-7.) Christians were forced to choose either to yield their integrity and accept the papal ceremonies and worship, or to wear away their lives in dungeon cells, or suffer death by the rack, the flame, or the headsman's ax. Now were fulfilled the words of Jesus, "You will be betrayed even by parents and brothers, relatives and friends; and they will put some of you to death. And you will be hated by all for My name's sake." Luke 21:16, 17. Persecution against the faithful began with greater fury than ever before, and the world became a vast battlefield. For hundreds of years the church of Christ found refuge in seclusion and obscurity. The prophet said, "Then the woman fled into the wilderness, where she has a place prepared by God, that they should feed her there one thousand two hundred and sixty days." Revelation 12:6.

The Dark Ages—The rise of the Roman Church to power marked the beginning of the Dark Ages. As her power increased, the darkness deepened. Faith was transferred from Christ, the true foundation, to the pope of Rome. Instead of trusting in the Son of God for forgiveness of sins and for eternal salvation, the people looked to the pope and to the priests and prelates to whom he delegated authority. They were taught that the pope was their mediator, and that none could approach God except through him, and further, that he stood in the place of God to them, and therefore must be obeyed implicitly. A deviation from his requirements was reason enough for the severest punishment to be inflicted on the bodies and souls of the offenders.

So the minds of the people were turned away from God to fallible, erring, and cruel men—and more than that, to the prince of darkness himself, who exercised his power through them. Sin was disguised in a garb of sanctity. When the Scriptures are suppressed, and human beings come to regard themselves as supreme, we need expect only fraud, deception, and debasing iniquity. Along with the elevation of human laws and traditions came the corruption that always results from setting aside the law of God.

Days of Peril—Those were days of peril for the church of Christ. The faithful standard-bearers were few indeed. Though the truth was not left without witnesses, yet at times it seemed that error and superstition would have total victory, and true religion would be banished from the earth. The church lost sight of the gospel, but the forms of religion were multiplied, and the people were burdened with rigorous requirements.

They were taught not only to look to the pope as their mediator but to trust to works of their own to atone for sin. Long pilgrimages, acts of penance, the worship of relics, the erection of churches, shrines, and altars, the payment of large sums to the church—these and many similar acts were commanded in order to appease the wrath of God or to secure his favor, as if God were like human beings, to be angered at trifles, or pacified by gifts or acts of penance!

The advancing centuries witnessed a constant increase of error in the doctrines put forth from Rome. Even before the establishment of the Papacy, the teachings of heathen philosophers had received attention and exerted an influence in the church. Many who professed conversion still clung to the principles of their pagan philosophy, and not only continued its study themselves but urged it upon others as a means of extending their influence among the heathen. This introduced serious errors into the Christian faith. Prominent among these was the belief in man's natural immortality and his consciousness in death. This doctrine laid the foundation on which Rome established praying to the saints and the adoration of the virgin Mary. From this sprung also the heresy of eternal torment for those who die without repenting, which was early incorporated into the papal faith.

These things prepared the way for introducing still another invention of paganism, which Rome named purgatory, and employed it to terrify the gullible and superstitious multitudes. This heresy affirmed the existence of a place of torment in which the souls of those who have not earned eternal damnation are to suffer punishment for their sins, and from which, after being freed from impurity, they are admitted to heaven.

Still another fabrication was needed to enable Rome to profit by the fears and the vices of her adherents. The doctrine of indulgences met this need. Full forgiveness of sins—past, present, and future—and release from all the pains and penalties incurred were promised to all who would enlist in the pontiff's wars to extend his temporal dominion, to punish his enemies, or to exterminate those who dared deny his spiritual supremacy. The people were also taught that by the payment of money to the church they might free themselves from sin and also release the souls of their deceased friends who were kept in the tormenting flames. By such means Rome filled her coffers and sustained the magnificence, luxury, and vice of the pretended representatives of Him who had nowhere to lay His head.

The Scriptural ordinance of the Lord's supper had been displaced by the idolatrous sacrifice of the mass. Priests pretended to convert the simple bread and wine into the actual body and blood of Christ. With blasphemous presumption they openly claimed the power to "create their Creator." On pain of death, all Christians were required to avow their faith in this horrible, Heaven-insulting heresy. Those who refused were given to the flames.

The noontide of the Papacy was the world's moral midnight. The Holy Scriptures were almost unknown, not only to the people, but to the priests. Like the Pharisees of old, the church leaders hated the light that would reveal their sins. Having removed God's law, the standard of righteousness, they exercised power without limit and practiced vice without restraint. Fraud, greed, and immorality prevailed. People shrank from no crime by which they could gain wealth or position. The palaces of popes and prelates were scenes of the vilest debauchery. Some of the reigning pontiffs were guilty of crimes so revolting that secular rulers tried to depose these dignitaries of the church as monsters too vile to be tolerated on the throne. For centuries there was no progress in learning, arts, or civilization. A moral and intellectual paralysis had fallen on Christendom.

Chapter 12

The Sanctuary

The Protestant Reformation arose to address many of the errors of Rome. The reformers also took up other matters, long neglected, that they found in Scripture. By the nineteenth century, interest in the second coming of Jesus was growing among Bible students of various denominations and countries. Many expected the event to happen in the first half of that century. The movement was especially strong in America, where its followers became known as "adventists." Based on a time prophecy in Daniel 8:14 about the cleansing of the sanctuary, they expected Jesus to come and cleanse the earth in 1844. When this did not happen, some of them searched the Bible to understand why.

The Earthly and Heavenly Sanctuaries—In their investigation these earnest Bible students learned that the earthly sanctuary, which Moses built at the command of God according to the pattern shown him on Mount Sinai, was "a figure for the time then present, in which were offered both gifts and sacrifices." Hebrews 9:9, KJV. They learned that its two holy places were "copies of the things in the heavens"; that Christ, our great High Priest, is "a Minister of the sanctuary and of the true tabernacle which the Lord erected, and not man"; and that "Christ has not entered the holy places made with hands, which are copies of the true, but into heaven itself, now to appear in the presence of God for us." Hebrews 9:23; 8:2; Hebrews 9:24.

The sanctuary in heaven, in which Jesus ministers in our behalf, is the great original, of which the sanctuary that Moses built was a copy. As the sanctuary on earth had two apartments or rooms, the holy and the most holy, so there are two holy places in the sanctuary in heaven. And the ark containing the law of God, the altar of incense, and other instruments of service found in the sanctuary below also have their counterpart in the sanctuary above. In holy vision the apostle John was permitted to enter heaven, and there he saw the candlestick or lampstand, and the altar of incense, and as "the temple of God was opened," he also saw "the ark of His covenant." Revelation 4:5; 8:3; Revelation 11:19.

Those who were seeking for the truth found indisputable proof that a sanctuary exists in heaven. Moses made the earthly sanctuary after a pattern shown to him. Paul declared that that pattern was the true sanctuary, which is in heaven (Hebrews 8:2, 5). John testified that he saw it in heaven.

At the end of the 2300 days, in 1844, no sanctuary had existed on earth for many centuries. Therefore, the sanctuary in heaven must be the one brought to view in the declaration, "For two thousand three hundred days; then the sanctuary shall be cleansed." Daniel 8:14. But how could the sanctuary in heaven need cleansing? Turning again to the Scriptures, the students of prophecy learned that the cleansing was not a removal of physical impurities, for it was to be accomplished with blood, and therefore it must be a cleansing from sin. The apostle says: "Therefore it was necessary that the copies of the things in the heavens should be purified with these [the blood of animals], but the heavenly things themselves with better sacrifices than these [even the precious blood of Christ]." Hebrews 9:23.

To obtain further knowledge of the cleansing to which the prophecy points, they needed to understand the services of the heavenly sanctuary. They could only learn this from the services of the earthly sanctuary, for Paul declares that the priests who officiated there served "the copy and shadow of the heavenly things." Hebrews 8:5.

The Cleansing of the Sanctuary—Anciently, as the sins of the people were transferred, in symbol, to the earthly sanctuary by the blood of the sin offering, so our sins are, in fact, transferred to the heavenly sanctuary by the blood of Christ. And as the symbolic cleansing of the earthly was accomplished by the removal of the sins that had polluted it, so the actual cleansing of the heavenly is to be accomplished by the removal, or blotting out, of the sins that are recorded there. This requires an examination of the books of record to determine who, through repentance of sin and faith in Christ, are entitled to the benefits of His atonement. The cleansing of the sanctuary therefore involves a work of investigative judgment. This work must be performed before the coming of Christ to redeem His people, because when He comes, His reward is with Him to give to every one according to his works. (Revelation 22:12.)

Thus those who followed in the advancing light of the prophetic word saw that instead of coming to the earth at the end of the 2300 days in 1844, Christ then entered the most holy place of the heavenly sanctuary, into the presence of God, to perform the closing work of atonement, in preparation for His coming.

A Solemn Message—When Christ entered the most holy place of the heavenly sanctuary to perform the closing work of the atonement, He entrusted His servants with the last message of mercy to be given to the world. This is the warning of the third angel of Revelation 14. The prophet sees that immediately following its proclamation, the Son of man is coming in glory to reap the harvest of the earth.

The most fearful threatening ever addressed to mortals is contained in the third angel's message (Revelation 14:9-12). It must be a terrible sin which calls down the wrath of God unmingled with mercy. People are not to be left in darkness concerning this important matter. The warning against this sin is to be given to the world before the arrival of God's judgments, that all may know why these judgments are to be inflicted and may have opportunity to escape them.

In the issue of the great contest, two distinct, opposite classes are developed. In one class is everyone who "worships the beast and his image, and receives his mark on his forehead or on his hand," and thus who bring upon themselves the awful judgments threatened by the third angel. The other class, in marked contrast to the world, are those who "keep the commandments of God and the faith of Jesus." Revelation 14:9, 12.

Chapter 13

The Deliverance

In this chapter and those that follow, the author writes of things that are still future, but often expresses them in past tense, like an eyewitness recounting events seen.

THE CLOSE OF PROBATION

When the third angel's message was closing, the power of God had rested upon His people. They had accomplished their work and were prepared for the trying hour before them. They had received the latter rain, or refreshing from the presence of the Lord, and the living testimony had been revived. The last great warning had sounded everywhere, and it had stirred up and enraged the inhabitants of the earth who would not receive the message.

Angels were hurrying to and fro in heaven. An angel with a writer's inkhorn by his side returned from the earth and reported to Jesus that his work was done, and the saved were numbered and sealed. Then Jesus, who had been ministering before the ark containing the Ten Commandments, threw down the censer. He raised His hands, and with a loud voice said, "It is done." And all the angels laid off their crowns as Jesus made the solemn declaration, "He who is unjust, let him be unjust still; he who is filthy, let him be filthy still; he who is righteous, let him be righteous still; he who is holy, let him be holy still." Revelation 22:11.

Every case had been decided for life or death. While Jesus had been ministering in the sanctuary, the judgment had been going on for the righteous dead, and then for the righteous living. Christ had received His kingdom, having made the atonement for His people and blotted out their sins. The subjects of the kingdom were determined. The marriage of the

Lamb was accomplished. And the kingdom, and the greatness of the kingdom under the whole heaven, was given to Jesus and the heirs of salvation, and Jesus was to reign as King of kings and Lord of lords.

As Jesus moved out of the most holy place, the bells on His garment tinkled; and as He left, a cloud of darkness covered the inhabitants of the earth. There was then no mediator between guilty humanity and an offended God. While Jesus had been standing between God and guilty humanity, a restraint was upon the people; but when He stepped out from between mankind and the Father, the restraint was removed, and Satan had entire control of those who refused to repent.

It was impossible for the plagues to be poured out while Jesus officiated in the sanctuary, but as His work there is finished and His intercession closes, there is nothing to hold back the wrath of God, and it breaks with fury on the shelterless head of the guilty sinner, who has made light of salvation and hated reproof. In that fearful time, after the close of Jesus' mediation, the people of God, whom the Bible calls saints, were living in the sight of a holy God without an intercessor. Every case was decided, every jewel numbered.

Too Late!—Then Jesus laid off His priestly attire and clothed Himself with His most kingly robes. On His head were many crowns, a crown within a crown. Surrounded by the angelic host, He left heaven. The plagues were falling on the inhabitants of the earth. Some were denouncing God and cursing Him. Others rushed to the people of God and begged to be taught how to escape His judgments. But the saints had nothing for them. The last tear for sinners had been shed, the last agonizing prayer offered, the last burden borne, the last warning given. The sweet voice of mercy was no longer inviting them. When the saints, and all heaven, were interested for their salvation, they had no interest for themselves. Life and death had been set before them. Many desired life but made no effort to obtain it. They did not choose life, and now there was no atoning blood to cleanse the guilty, no compassionate

Savior to plead for them and cry, "Spare, spare the sinner a little longer." All heaven had united with Jesus as they heard the fearful words, "It is done! It is finished!" The plan of salvation had been accomplished, but few had chosen to accept it. And as mercy's sweet voice died away, fear and horror seized the wicked. With terrible distinctness they heard the words, "Too late! too late!"

Many of the wicked were greatly enraged as they suffered the effects of the plagues in fearful agony. Parents were bitterly blaming their children, and children their parents, brothers their sisters, and sisters their brothers. Loud, wailing cries came from every direction: "It was you who kept me from receiving the truth that would have saved me from this awful hour." The people turned on their ministers with bitter hate and blamed them, saying, "You have not warned us. You told us that all the world was to be converted, and you cried, Peace, peace, to quiet every fear that was aroused. You have not told us of this hour; and those who warned us of it you declared to be fanatics and evil people, who would ruin us." But the ministers did not escape the wrath of God. Their suffering was tenfold greater than that of their people.

THE TIME OF JACOB'S TROUBLE

The saints left the cities and villages and associated together in companies, living in the most solitary places. Angels provided them food and water, while the wicked were suffering from hunger and thirst. The leading men of the earth consulted together, with Satan and his angels busy around them. Copies of a writing were scattered in different parts of the land, giving orders that unless the saints would yield their distinct faith, give up the Sabbath, and observe the first day of the week, the people were free after a certain time to kill them. But in this trying time the saints were calm and composed, trusting in God and leaning on His promise that a way of escape would be made for them.

In some places, before the time for the decree to be executed, the wicked rushed on the saints to kill them, but Jesus commanded His angels to watch over them. God would be honored by making a covenant with those who had kept His law, in the sight of their enemies surrounding them; and Jesus would be honored by translating the faithful, waiting ones who had expected Him for so long, without their experiencing death.

The saints were suffering great mental anguish. They seemed to be surrounded by the wicked inhabitants of the earth. Everything appeared to be against them. Some began to fear that God had finally left them to die by the hand of the wicked. But if their eyes could have been opened, they would have seen themselves surrounded by angels of God. Next came the mob of the angry wicked, and next a mass of evil angels, hurrying the wicked on to kill the saints. But before they could approach God's people, the wicked must first pass this company of mighty, holy angels. This was impossible. The angels of God were causing them to recede and also causing the evil angels who were pressing around them to fall back.

The Cry for Deliverance—It was a time of fearful, terrible agony to the saints. Day and night they cried to God for deliverance. To outward appearance, there was no possibility of their escape. The wicked had already begun to triumph, taunting them: "Why doesn't your God deliver you out of our hands? Why don't you go up and save your lives?" But the saints did not listen to them. Like Jacob, they were wrestling with God (Genesis 32:22-32). The angels longed to deliver them, but they must wait a little longer. The people of God must drink from the cup and be baptized with the baptism of great trial. The angels continued their watch, faithful to their trust. God would not allow His name to be dishonored among the heathen. The time had nearly come when He was to display His mighty power and gloriously deliver His saints. For His name's glory He would deliver every one of those who had patiently waited for Him and whose names were written in the book.

It was like the experience of faithful Noah. When the rain

fell and the Flood came, Noah and his family had entered the ark, and God had shut them in. Noah had faithfully warned the inhabitants of the pre-Flood world, while they had mocked and derided him. And as the waters came down on the earth, and one after another was drowning, they saw that ark, which they had ridiculed, riding safely on the waters, preserving the faithful Noah and his family. It was no less sure that at the end of time the people of God, who had faithfully warned the world of His coming wrath, would be delivered. God would not allow the wicked to destroy those who were expecting translation and who would not bow to the decree of the beast or receive his mark. If the wicked were permitted to kill the saints, Satan and all his evil angels, and all who hate God, would be gratified. And oh, what a triumph it would be in the last closing struggle for his satanic majesty to have power over those who had so long waited to see Jesus, whom they loved! Those who have mocked at the idea of the saints' going up will witness the care God has for His people and see their glorious deliverance.

As the saints left the cities and villages, they were pursued by the wicked, who tried to kill them. But the weapons that were raised to kill God's people broke and fell as powerless as straw. Angels of God shielded the saints. As they cried day and night for deliverance, their cry came up before the Lord.

Deliverance of the Saints

It was at midnight when God chose to deliver His people. As the wicked were mocking around them, suddenly the sun appeared, shining in its strength, and the moon stood still. The wicked looked at the scene with amazement, while with solemn joy the saints saw the first indications of their deliverance. Signs and wonders followed in quick succession. Everything seemed turned out of its natural course. The streams ceased to flow. Dark, heavy clouds came up and clashed against each other. But there was one clear place of settled glory, and from it came the voice of God like many waters, shaking the heavens and the earth. There was a mighty earthquake. The graves were opened, and those who had died in faith under the third angel's message, keeping the Sabbath, came out from their dusty beds glorified, to hear the covenant of peace that God was to make with those who had kept His law.

The sky opened and shut and was in commotion. The mountains shook like a reed in the wind and scattered ragged rocks all around. The sea boiled like a pot and cast out stones on the land. And as God delivered the everlasting covenant to His people, He spoke one sentence, and then paused, while the words were rolling through the earth. The Israel of God stood with their eyes fixed upward, listening to the words as they came from the mouth of Jehovah and rolled through the earth like peals of loudest thunder. It was awfully solemn. At the end of every sentence the saints shouted, "Glory! Hallelujah!" Their countenances were lighted up with the glory of God, shining with glory like the face of Moses did when he came down from Sinai. The wicked could not look at them because of the glory. And when God pronounced the never-ending blessing on those who had honored Him in keeping His Sabbath holy, they gave a mighty shout of victory over the beast and over his image.

The Second Advent of Christ—Soon appeared the great white cloud, on which sat the Son of man. When it first appeared in the distance, this cloud looked very small. As it drew nearer the earth, everyone could see the excellent glory and majesty of Jesus as He rode onward to conquer. A retinue of holy angels with bright, glittering crowns on their heads escorted Him on His way.

No language can describe the glory of the scene. The living cloud of majesty and unsurpassed glory came still nearer, on which was the lovely person of Jesus, not wearing a crown of thorns, but a crown of glory on His holy brow. On His robe and thigh was a name written, King of kings, and Lord of lords (Revelation 19:16). His face was as bright as the noon-day sun, His eyes were as a flame of fire, and His feet had the appearance of fine brass (Revelation 1:14-16). His voice sounded like many musical instruments. The earth trembled in His presence, the heavens departed as a scroll when it is rolled together, and every mountain and island were moved out of their places. "And the kings of the earth, the great men, the rich men, the commanders, the mighty men, every slave and every free man, hid themselves in the caves and in the rocks of the mountains, and said to the mountains and rocks, 'Fall on us and hide us from the face of Him who sits on the throne and from the wrath of the Lamb! For the great day of His wrath has come, and who is able to stand?' " Revelation 6:15-17.

Those who a short time before would have destroyed God's faithful children from the earth now witnessed the glory of God resting on them. And amid all their terror they heard the voices of the saints in joyful sounds, saying, "Behold, this is our God; we have waited for Him, and He will save us." Isaiah 25:9.

The First Resurrection—The earth shook mightily as the voice of the Son of God called the sleeping saints from their graves. They responded to the call and came up clothed with glorious immortality, crying, "Victory, victory, over death and the grave! O death, where is thy sting? O grave, where is thy victory?" (See 1 Corinthians 15:55, KJV.) Then the living saints and the risen ones raised their voices in a long, ecstatic shout of victory. Those bodies that had gone down into the grave carrying the marks of disease and death came up in immortal health and vigor. The living saints are changed in a moment, in the twinkling of an eye, and caught up with the risen ones, and together they meet their Lord in the air. Oh, what a glorious meeting! Friends whom death had separated were united, never to part again.

On each side of the cloudy chariot were wings, and beneath it were living wheels. And the saints in the cloud cried, "Glory! Alleluia!" And the chariot rolled upward to the Holy City. Before entering the city, the saints were arranged in a perfect square, with Jesus in the midst. He stood head and shoulders above the saints and above the angels. All in the square could see His majestic form and lovely face.

THE SAINTS' REWARD

Then from the city a very great number of angels brought glorious crowns—a crown for every saint, with his name written on it. As Jesus called for the crowns, angels presented them to Him; and with His own right hand Jesus placed the crowns on the heads of the saints. In the same manner the angels brought the harps, and Jesus presented them also to the saints. The commanding angels first struck the note, and then every voice was raised in grateful, happy praise, and every hand skillfully swept over the strings of the harp, sending forth melodious music in rich and perfect tones.

Then Jesus led the redeemed company to the gate of the city. He laid hold of the gate, swung it back on its glittering hinges, and invited the nations that had kept the truth to enter in. Within the city there was everything for the eye to feast on. Rich glory they beheld everywhere. Then Jesus looked at His redeemed saints, with their faces radiant with glory. As He fixed His loving eyes on them, He said, with His rich, musical voice, "I am seeing the travail of My soul, and I am satisfied. This rich glory is yours to enjoy eternally. Your sorrows are ended. There will be no more death, neither sorrow nor crying, neither shall there be any more pain." The redeemed bowed and laid their glittering crowns at the feet of Jesus, and then, as His lovely hand raised them up, they touched their golden harps and filled all heaven with their rich music and songs to the Lamb.

Then Jesus led His people to the tree of life, and again they heard His beautiful voice, richer than any music that ever fell on mortal ear, saying, "The leaves of this tree are for the healing of the nations. Eat from it, all of you." On the tree of life was most beautiful fruit, of which the saints could eat freely. In the city was a most glorious throne, and proceeding out from it was a pure river of water of life, clear as crystal. On each side of this river was the tree of life, and on the banks of the river were other beautiful trees bearing fruit that was good for food.

Language is altogether too feeble to attempt a description of heaven. We can only exclaim, "Oh, what love! what wondrous love!" The most exalted language fails to describe the glory of heaven or the matchless depths of a Savior's love.

Chapter 14

The Sentence

THE MILLENNIUM

On the earth, the wicked had been destroyed, and their dead bodies were lying on its surface. The wrath of God in the seven last plagues had come upon the inhabitants of the earth, causing them to gnaw their tongues from pain and to curse God. After the saints had been delivered by the voice of God, the wicked multitude turned their rage on one another. The earth seemed to be deluged with blood, and dead bodies were from one end of it to the other.

The earth looked like a desolate wilderness. Cities and villages, shaken down by the earthquake, lay in heaps. Mountains had been moved out of their places, leaving large caverns. Ragged rocks, thrown out by the sea, or torn out of the earth itself, were scattered all over its surface. Large uprooted trees were strewn over the land. Here is to be the home of Satan with his evil angels for a thousand years. Here he will be confined, to wander up and down over the broken surface of the earth and see the effects of his rebellion against God's law. For a thousand years he can enjoy the fruit of the curse that he has caused.

Confined alone to the earth, he will not have the privilege of ranging to other worlds, to tempt and annoy those who have not fallen. During this time Satan suffers extremely. Since his fall his evil traits have been in constant use. But during these thousand years he will be deprived of his power and left to reflect on the part he has acted since his fall, and to look forward with trembling and terror to the dreadful future when he must suffer for all the evil that he has done and be punished for all the sins that he has caused to be committed.

From the angels and from the redeemed saints came shouts

of triumph like ten thousand musical instruments, because Satan would never again annoy and tempt them and because the inhabitants of other worlds were delivered from his presence and his temptations.

Jesus and the redeemed saints sat upon thrones, and the saints reigned as kings and priests unto God. Christ, in union with His people, judged the wicked dead, comparing their acts with the Statute Book, the Word of God, and deciding every case according to the deeds done in the body. (See Revelation 20:4-6.) Then they allotted to the wicked the portion that they must suffer, according to their works, and it was written against their names in the book of death. Jesus and the saints also judged Satan and his angels. Satan's punishment would be far greater than that of those he had deceived. His suffering would so far exceed theirs as to bear no comparison with it. After all those whom he had deceived had perished, Satan was still to live and suffer on much longer.

After the judgment of the wicked dead was finished, at the end of the thousand years, Jesus left the city, and the saints and a retinue of angels followed Him. Jesus descended onto a great mountain, and as soon as His feet touched it, it split and became a wide plain. Then the great and beautiful city, with twelve foundations and twelve gates, three on each side, and an angel at each gate, appeared above. The redeemed cried out, "The city! the great city! It is coming down from God out of heaven!" And it came down in all its splendor and dazzling glory, and settled in the mighty plain that Jesus had prepared for it.

The Second Resurrection—Then, in terrible, fearful majesty, Jesus called the wicked dead back to life. They came up with the same feeble, sickly bodies that went into the grave. What a scene! Those in the first resurrection had all come up in immortal bloom, but in the second resurrection the marks of the curse are visible on all. The kings and noblemen of the earth, the poor and low, the educated and uneducated, come from the grave together. They all see the Son of man.

Those very men who despised and mocked Him, who put the crown of thorns on His sacred brow and struck Him with the reed, see Him now in all His kingly majesty. Those who spat on Him in the hour of His trial now turn from His piercing gaze and from the glory of His face. Those who drove the nails through His hands and feet now look on the marks of His crucifixion. Those who thrust the spear into His side see the marks of their cruelty on His body. And they know that He is the very one whom they crucified and derided in His dying agony. And then there arises one long, protracted wail of agony, as they flee to hide from the presence of the King of kings and Lord of lords.

All are seeking to hide in the rocks, to shield themselves from the terrible glory of Him whom they once despised. And, overwhelmed and pained with His majesty and great glory, they raise their voices together, and with terrible distinctness exclaim, "Blessed is He who comes in the name of the Lord!"

Then Jesus and the holy angels, with all the saints, again go to the city, and the bitter cries and wailings of the doomed wicked fill the air. Then Satan again began his work. He went around among his subjects and made the weak and feeble strong, telling them that he and his angels were powerful. He pointed to the countless millions who had been raised. There were mighty warriors and kings who were well skilled in battle and who had conquered kingdoms. And there were mighty giants and valiant men who had never lost a battle. There was the proud, ambitious Napoleon, whose approach had caused kingdoms to tremble. Men of lofty stature and dignified bearing were there, who had fallen in battle while thirsting to conquer.

As they come from their graves, they resume the current of their thoughts where it stopped in death. They have the same desire to conquer that ruled them when they fell. Satan consults with his angels and then with those kings and conquerors and mighty men. Then he looks over the vast army and tells them that the company in the city is small and feeble, and that they can go up and take it, and throw its inhabitants out, and possess its riches and glory themselves.

Satan succeeds in deceiving them, and immediately they all begin to prepare themselves for battle. There are many skillful men in that vast army, and they construct all kinds of implements of war. Then with Satan at their head, the multitude moves on. Kings and warriors follow close after Satan, and the horde follows after in companies. Each company has its leader, and in orderly fashion they march over the broken surface of the earth to the Holy City. Jesus closes the gates of the city, and soldiers of this vast army surround it and place themselves in battle array, expecting a fierce conflict.

THE CORONATION OF CHRIST

Now Christ again comes into the view of His enemies. Far above the city, on a foundation of burnished gold, is a throne, high and lifted up. On this throne sits the Son of God, and around Him are the subjects of His kingdom. No language can describe the power and majesty of Christ; no pen can portray it. The glory of the Eternal Father enshrouds His Son. The brightness of His presence fills the city of God and flows out beyond the gates, flooding the whole earth with its radiance.

Nearest the throne are those who once were zealous in the cause of Satan, but who, plucked like brands from the burning, have followed their Savior with deep, intense devotion. Next are those who perfected Christian characters in the midst of falsehood and unbelief, those who honored the law of God when the Christian world said it was void, and the millions, of all ages, who were martyred for their faith. And beyond is the "great multitude which no one could number, of all nations, tribes, peoples, and tongues, standing before the throne and before the Lamb, clothed with white robes, with palm branches in their hands." Revelation 7:9. Their warfare is ended, their victory won. They have run the race and reached the prize. The palm branch in their hands is a symbol of their triumph, and the white robe an emblem of the spotless righteousness of Christ, which now is theirs.

The redeemed raise a song of praise that echoes and re-echoes through the vaults of heaven: "Salvation belongs to our God who sits on the throne, and to the Lamb!" And angels unite their voices in adoration. As the redeemed have witnessed the power and evil intent of Satan, they have seen, as never before, that no power but that of Christ could have made them conquerors. In all that shining company there are none to take the credit for salvation to themselves, as if they had prevailed by their own power and goodness. They have nothing to say about what they have done or suffered, but the burden of every song, the keynote of every anthem, is, "Salvation belongs to our God . . . and to the Lamb!" Revelation 7:10.

In the presence of the assembled inhabitants of earth and heaven, the final coronation of the Son of God takes place. And now, invested with supreme majesty and power, the King of kings pronounces sentence on the rebels against His government and executes justice on those who have transgressed His law and oppressed His people. Says the prophet of God: "I saw a great white throne and Him who sat on it, from whose face the earth and the heaven fled away. And there was found no place for them. And I saw the dead, small and great, standing before God, and books were opened. And another book was opened, which is the Book of Life. And the dead were judged according to their works, by the things which were written in the books." Revelation 20:11, 12.

As soon as the books of record are opened, and the eye of Jesus looks at the wicked, they are conscious of every sin that they have ever committed. They see just where their feet strayed from the path of purity and holiness, just how far pride and rebellion have carried them in violating the law of God. The seductive temptations that they encouraged by indulgence in sin, the blessings they perverted, the waves of mercy beaten back by the stubborn, unrepentant heart—all appear as if written in letters of fire.

Panorama of the Great Conflict—Above the throne they see the cross, and the scenes of Adam's temptation and fall and the successive steps in the great plan of redemption appear like a panoramic view. The Savior's lowly birth, His early life of simplicity and obedience, His baptism in the Jordan, the fasting and temptation in the wilderness, His public ministry that offered men and women heaven's most precious blessings, the days crowded with deeds of love and mercy, the nights of prayer and watching in the solitude of the mountains, the plottings of envy, hate, and malice that repaid His benefits, the awful mysterious agony in Gethsemane beneath the crushing weight of the sins of the whole world, His betrayal into the hands of the murderous mob, the fearful events of that night of horror: the unresisting prisoner, forsaken by His best-loved disciples, rudely hurried through the streets of Jerusalem, the Son of God exultingly displayed before Annas, arraigned in the high priest's palace, in the judgment hall of Pilate, before the cowardly and cruel Herod, mocked, insulted, tortured, and condemned to die—all are vividly portrayed.

And now before the swaying multitude the final scenes are revealed: the patient Sufferer treading the path to Calvary, the Prince of heaven hanging on the cross, the haughty priests and the jeering rabble deriding His dying agony, the supernatural darkness, the heaving earth, the split rocks, the open graves, marking the moment when the world's Redeemer yielded up His life.

The awful spectacle appears just as it was. Satan, his angels, and his followers have no power to turn away from the picture of their own work. Each actor recalls the part that he performed. Herod, who killed the innocent children of Bethlehem in an effort to destroy the King of Israel; the evil Herodias, on whose guilty soul rests the blood of John the Baptist; the weak, time-serving Pilate; the mocking soldiers; the priests and rulers and the maddened mob who cried, "His blood be on us, and on our children"—all understand how enormous their guilt is. They try unsuccessfully to hide from the divine majesty of His face, outshining the glory of the sun, while the redeemed put their crowns at the Savior's feet, exclaiming, "He died for me!"

Among the redeemed are the apostles of Christ, the heroic Paul, the ardent Peter, the loved and loving John, and their truehearted brethren, and with them the vast legion of martyrs, while outside the walls, with every vile and abominable thing, are those who persecuted, imprisoned, and killed them. There is Nero, that monster of cruelty and vice, seeing the joy and honor of those he once tortured, and in whose extreme anguish he found Satanic delight. His mother is there to witness the result of her own work, to see how the evil stamp of character she transmitted to her son, the passions encouraged and developed by her influence and example, have borne fruit in crimes that caused the world to shudder.

There are priests and prelates who claimed to be Christ's ambassadors, yet employed the rack, the dungeon, and the stake to control the consciences of His people. There are the proud pontiffs who exalted themselves above God and presumed to change the law of the Most High. Those pretended fathers of the church have an account to render to God, from which they would gladly be excused. Too late they will see that the Omniscient One is jealous for His law, and that He will not clear the guilty. They learn now that Christ identifies with His suffering people, and they feel the force of His own words, "Inasmuch as you did it to one of the least of these My brethren, you did it to Me." Matthew 25:40.

At the Bar of Judgment—The whole wicked world stands arraigned at the judgment bar of God, on the charge of high treason against the government of heaven. The lost have none to plead their case. They are without excuse, and the sentence of eternal death is pronounced against them.

It is now clear to all that the wages of sin is not noble independence and eternal life, but slavery, ruin, and death. The wicked see what they have lost by their life of rebellion. They despised the "far more exceeding and eternal weight of glory" when it was offered them, but how desirable it now appears.

"All this," cries the lost soul, "I might have had, but I chose to put these things far from me. Oh, strange infatuation! I have exchanged peace, happiness, and honor for wretchedness, shame, and despair." All see that their exclusion from heaven is just. In their lives they declared, We will not have this Jesus to reign over us.

As if entranced, the wicked have gazed at the coronation of the Son of God. They see in His hands the tablets of the divine law, the statutes that they have despised and transgressed. They witness the outburst of wonder, joy, and adoration from the saved, and as the wave of melody sweeps over the ranks outside the city, all with one voice exclaim, "Marvelous are Your works, Lord God Almighty! Just and true are Your ways, O King of the saints" (Revelation 15:3), and falling face down, they worship the Prince of life.

The Second Death—Satan seems paralyzed as he sees the glory and majesty of Christ. He who was once a covering cherub remembers from where he has fallen. A shining angel, "son of the morning"—how changed, how degraded!

Satan sees that his voluntary rebellion has made him unfit for heaven. He has trained his powers to war against God, so the purity, peace, and harmony of heaven would be to him supreme torture. His accusations against the mercy and justice of God are now silenced. The blame that he has tried to cast on Jehovah rests entirely on himself. And now Satan bows down and confesses the justice of his sentence.

Every question of truth and error in the long controversy is made plain. God's justice stands fully vindicated. The whole world has seen a clear presentation of the great sacrifice the Father and the Son made in mankind's behalf. The hour has come when Christ occupies His rightful position and is glorified above principalities and powers and every name that is named.

Even though Satan has been forced to acknowledge God's justice and to bow to the supremacy of Christ, his character remains unchanged. The spirit of rebellion, like a mighty river, bursts out again. Filled with frenzy, he determines not to yield the great controversy. The time has come for a last desperate struggle against the King of heaven. He rushes in among his subjects and tries to inspire them with his own fury and arouse them to instant battle. But of all the countless millions whom he has lured into rebellion, there are none now to acknowledge his supremacy. His power is at an end. The wicked are filled with the same hatred of God that inspires Satan, but they see that their case is hopeless, that they cannot win against Jehovah. They become enraged against Satan and those who have been his agents in deception. With the fury of demons they turn upon them, and there follows a scene of universal strife.

Then are fulfilled the words of the prophet: "The indignation of the Lord is against all nations, and His fury against all their armies; He has utterly destroyed them, He has given them over to the slaughter." Isaiah 34:2. "Upon the wicked He will rain coals; fire and brimstone and a burning wind shall be the portion of their cup." Psalm 11:6. Fire comes down from God out of heaven. The earth is broken up. The weapons of nature concealed in its depths are drawn out. Devouring flames burst from every yawning chasm. The very rocks are on fire. The day has come that will be "burning like an oven." Malachi 4:1. The elements melt with fervent heat, and both the earth and the works that are in it are burned up. (2 Peter 3:10.) The earth's surface seems one molten mass—a vast, seething lake of fire. It is the time of the judgment and destruction of the ungodly—"the day of the Lord's vengeance, the year of recompense for the cause of Zion." Isaiah 34:8.

The wicked receive their just reward in the earth. They " 'will be stubble. And the day which is coming shall burn them up,' says the Lord of hosts." Malachi 4:1. Some are destroyed as in a moment, while others suffer many days. All are punished according to their deeds. Satan is made to suffer, not only for his own rebellion, but for all the sins he has caused God's people to commit. His punishment is to be far greater than that of those whom he has deceived. After all have perished who fell by his deceptions, he is still to live and suffer on. In the cleansing flames the wicked are at last destroyed, root and branch—Satan the root, his followers the branches. The justice of God is satisfied, and the saints and all the angels say with a loud voice, Amen.

While the earth is wrapped in the fire of God's vengeance, the righteous are safe in the Holy City. Upon those who had part in the first resurrection, the second death has no power. (Revelation 20:6.) While God is to the wicked a consuming fire, He is to His people both a sun and a shield (Psalm 84:11).

Chapter 15

The New Beginning

"Now I saw a new heaven and a new earth, for the first heaven and the first earth had passed away." Revelation 21:1. The fire that consumes the wicked purifies the earth. Every trace of the curse is swept away. No eternally burning hell will keep the fearful consequences of sin before the saved. One reminder alone remains: our Redeemer will always carry the marks of His crucifixion. On His wounded head, His hands and feet, are the only traces of the cruel work that sin has done.

"O tower of the flock, the stronghold of the daughter of Zion, to you shall it come, even the former dominion shall come." Micah 4:8. The kingdom forfeited by sin, Christ has regained, and the redeemed are to possess it with Him. "The righteous shall inherit the land, and dwell in it forever." Psalm 37:29. A fear of making the saints' inheritance seem too material has led many to spiritualize away the very truths that lead us to look on the new earth as our home. Christ assured His disciples that He went to prepare places for them. Those who accept the teachings of God's Word will not be completely ignorant about their heavenly home. And yet the apostle Paul declares, "Eye has not seen, nor ear heard, nor have entered into the heart of man the things which God has prepared for those who love Him." 1 Corinthians 2:9. Human language is inadequate to describe the reward of the righteous. It will be known only to those who actually see it. No finite mind can comprehend the glory of the Paradise of God.

In the Bible the inheritance of the saved is called a country. (Hebrews 11:14-16.) There the great Shepherd leads His flock to fountains of living water. The tree of life yields its fruit every month, and the leaves of the tree are for the service of the nations. There are ever-flowing streams, clear as crystal, and beside them waving trees cast their shadows on the paths prepared for the ransomed of the Lord. There the wide-spreading plains swell into hills of beauty, and the mountains of God raise their lofty summits. On those peaceful plains, beside those living streams, God's people, who for so long have been pilgrims and wanderers, will find a home.

The New Jerusalem—There is the New Jerusalem, "having the glory of God," her light "like a most precious stone, like a jasper stone, clear as crystal." Revelation 21:11. Says the Lord, "I will rejoice in Jerusalem, and joy in My people." Isaiah 65:19. "The tabernacle of God is with men, and He will dwell with them, and they shall be His people. God Himself will be with them and be their God. And God will wipe away every tear from their eyes; there shall be no more death, nor sorrow, nor crying. There shall be no more pain, for the former things have passed away." Revelation 21:3, 4.

In the city of God "there shall be no night." No one will need or desire rest. There will be no weariness in doing the will of God and offering praise to His name. We will always feel the freshness of the morning, and will always be far from its close. "They need no lamp nor light of the sun, for the Lord God gives them light." Revelation 22:5. The light of the sun will be superseded by a radiance that is not painfully dazzling, yet which immeasurably surpasses the brightness of our noon. The glory of God and the Lamb floods the holy city with unfading light. The redeemed walk in the sunless glory of perpetual day.

"I saw no temple in it, for the Lord God Almighty and the Lamb are its temple." Revelation 21:22. The people of God are privileged to hold open fellowship with the Father and the Son. Now we "see in a mirror, dimly." 1 Corinthians 13:12. We behold the image of God reflected, as in a mirror, in the works of nature and in His dealings with people, but then we will see Him face to face, without a dimming veil between. We will stand in His presence and gaze on the glory of His face.

There immortal minds will study with never-failing delight the wonders of creative power, the mysteries of redeeming love. There is no cruel, deceiving enemy to tempt us to forget God. Every faculty will be developed, every capacity increased. Acquiring knowledge will not tire the mind or exhaust the energies. There the grandest undertakings may be carried forward, the loftiest aspirations reached, the highest ambitions realized, and still there will be new heights to climb, new wonders to admire, new truths to comprehend, fresh objects to draw out the powers of mind and soul and body.

And as the years of eternity roll, they will bring richer and more glorious revelations of God and of Christ. As knowledge is progressive, so will love, reverence, and happiness increase. The more people learn of God, the more they will admire His character. As Jesus opens before them the riches of redemption and the amazing achievements in the great controversy with Satan, the hearts of the ransomed beat with a stronger devotion, and they sweep the golden harps with a firmer hand; and ten thousand times ten thousand and thousands of thousands of voices unite to swell the mighty chorus of praise.

"And every creature which is in heaven and on the earth and under the earth and such as are in the sea, and all that are in them, I heard saying: 'Blessing and honor and glory and power be to Him who sits on the throne, and to the Lamb, forever and ever!' " Revelation 5:13.

Sin and sinners are no more. God's entire universe is clean, and the great controversy is forever ended.

Offering **God's good news** for a better life
today and for eternity

hopetv.org
Christian television programing about faith,
health, relationships, and community

Hope
CHANNEL

FREE Lessons at www.BibleStudies.com

Call:
1-888-456-7933

Write:
Discover
P.O. Box 999
Loveland, CO 80539-0999

It's easy to learn more about the Bible!